I dedicate this book not only to my treasure of family and friends, but also to all the animals I have had the privilege to know and love. Thank you all for your encouragement and unconditional love.

And this goes for Boo Boo Kitty too!

jest (jest) *n.* 1. To act or speak in a playful manner

Shirley,
I
Jest!

Shirley, I Jest!

A STORIED LIFE

CINDY WILLIAMS

with Dave Smitherman

Guilford, Connecticut

Use of photos from *Laverne & Shirley*—Courtesy of CBS Television Studios

An imprint of Globe Pequot

Distributed by NATIONAL BOOK NETWORK

British Library Cataloguing in Publication Information Available

Library of Congress Cataloging-in-Publication Data

The hardback edition of this book was previously cataloged by the Library of Congress as follows:

Williams, Cindy, 1947 August 22-
Shirley, I Jest! : a storied life / Cindy Williams.
pages cm
1. Williams, Cindy, 1947 August 22- 2. Actors—United States—Biography. I. Title.
PN2287.W465A3 2015
791.4302'8092—dc23
[B]   2014042840

ISBN 978-1-63076-012-0 (cloth : alk. paper)
ISBN 978-1-63076-268-1 (pbk. : alk. paper)
ISBN 978-1-63076-013-7 (electronic)

♾™ The paper used in this publication meets the minimum requirements of American National Standard for Information Sciences—Permanence of Paper for Printed Library Materials, ANSI/NISO Z39.48-1992.

Printed in the United States of America

Contents

Foreword
Ed Begley Jr.

America fell in love with Cindy Williams in 1977, when she began her hit show *Laverne & Shirley*. But, I fell in love with her seven years prior to that, at the wrap party for *Room 222*.

Though ours was never the romantic relationship I had hoped for after that first meeting, it wasn't for lack of trying. Our first date consisted of me picking her up in a three-wheel 1970 electric vehicle, which was not exactly a babe magnet. It was so slow that a kid on a scooter passed us by and gave us the finger. I decided to bide my time and wait for the right moment to pounce on her, but that didn't work out so well either.

I lulled her into a false sense of security, and convinced her to spend a weekend with me at Two Bunch Palms. After two years of waiting, I had little pride remaining. I did what any red-blooded male would do under those conditions. I begged her to let me into her room in hopes of getting to first base. I tried her door. Locked! And she probably had it bolted from inside. I thought about going around back to "jimmy" the window, but then the police might get involved. No, I had to make my peace with it. I had long ago

Foreword

become like a brother to her, and after weeping and begging, I quickly surmised that being her "brother" was a pretty sweet deal.

Her generosity in my life was endless. She became one of the biggest champions of my work as an actor, a stand-up comic, and an environmentalist. She loaned me a huge sum of money so I could buy my first house. She introduced me to a holistic doctor who kept me healthy for decades. She became the godmother to my daughter, Amanda. She got me cast as her brother on *Laverne & Shirley*. She introduced me to a long list of brilliant and creative people that are still an important part of my life.

We saved trees together, went on trips together, broke down on the highway together, and had many fantastic adventures together.

Though it wasn't what I had in mind at first, being considered "family" by this talented and dynamic woman is simply wonderful.

I suppose I should pay her back the money I borrowed.

Photo by Tricia Lee Pascoe

ONE

Valley Texas Gal

I gingerly opened the door to the smoke-filled Green Room at the Pasadena Playhouse and immediately started coughing. Everyone seemed to have a lit cigarette except for Betty Garrett and Cyd Charisse, who were sitting on a couch, chatting. I caught a glimpse of Frank Sinatra and Liza Minnelli sharing a laugh. Lucille Ball and her husband, Gary Morton, were playing mah-jongg. I made a hasty retreat, shutting the door quickly, hoping no one saw me. My coughing subsided, but now my head was spinning. How could they be so calm, carefree, and collected while I was having a full-blown anxiety attack? It was 1978; Laverne & Shirley was a huge success and I should have had the confidence of a gladiator. The corridor seemed to be swaying back and forth. Afraid I was going to faint, I leaned against the wall for support and dropped like a bag of bricks straight to the floor! I had leaned into a clothing rack by mistake. How had I gotten myself into this? In less than an hour I would step out onto the stage at the Pasadena Playhouse and sing "You Wonderful You" from the movie Summer Stock *as a duet with Gene*

Kelly. My mouth was dry. How would I ever be able to sing, let alone on key? My heart was pounding like a sledgehammer.

Even as a little girl I suffered from anxiety. My mother was always telling me to stop biting my nails, or commenting on how I could never sit still. In school I was punished for not being able to keep quiet. One time in second grade, I had to sit on a stool in the corner with a dunce cap on my head for talking too much and too loud. I was also painfully shy, which seems contradictory, but it's true. As much as I wanted to socialize and be a leader, a part of me resisted. Still, there was another ever-present part of me that longed to express the fantastic things I was imagining, share the fun of my shadow world—loudly and with exuberance. This is what earned me the dunce cap.

I started life in Van Nuys, California, in the San Fernando Valley. I'm what you might call a "Valley Girl." When I was born I had rickets; a vitamin D deficiency that affects the bones. My mother, Frances, loved to tell the story as though it were the Holy Grail of medical riddles. She would say,

> Rickets, of all things. Your little legs were bowed and I had to give you goat's milk, because you couldn't tolerate cow's milk. You also had the colic, poor little thing . . . crying and throwing up all the time. I labored for thirty-six hours. They finally knocked me out with ether, and then used the forceps on you.

(I have always blamed this use of forceps at my birth for my egg-shaped head!) My mother vigilantly researched this condition and eventually got me over it. And as a result, she started taking an avid interest in health and preventative medicine, ultimately becoming a lifelong devotee of Jack LaLanne and other health gurus. She collected tomes on the subject of wellness, and if anyone around her had a health complaint, she would check their tongue and skin coloring and then look it up. She became excellent at diagnosing and suggesting remedies for any maladies that crossed her path. Frances was ahead of her time.

My father's name was Beachard Williams, but he liked to be called Bill; which was odd because that was his brother's name. His family was from Texas and Louisiana. Their origins were Welsh, French, and Cherokee. My father was the kindest man I've ever known—fun-loving and affable—until he was drinking. When he drank he became the devil, and a very dangerous character to deal with. When I was a year old my mother left my father because of his drinking and aggressive behavior. We took the train to live with my grandmother Anna in Dallas, Texas, where my mother and father had met years before.

My grandmother was Sicilian and had emigrated with her younger brother Joe from "The Old Country" to America by way of Ellis Island and into Manhattan where my mother and her brother, Sam, were born. My grandfather had died falling off a truck on the way home from a winning streak in a poker game. My grandmother swore he had been pushed. Murdered by the Black Hand. When my mother was seven, my grandmother moved her family from Manhattan to Dallas, Texas, where her brother Joe had gone to live earlier.

After a year of living peacefully with my grandmother, my father showed up, and begged my mother to get back together. She agreed and the next year my sister, Carol, was born and we all lived together with my grandmother in her house on Poplar Street.

My brother, Jimmy, is seventeen years older than me. He is my mother's son from her first marriage and had already fled to our grandmother's house in Dallas to escape the drunken abuse my father would sometimes direct his way. When Jimmy was eighteen, he joined the Air Force and was out of the house for good.

Everyone worked during the day. My mother waitressed at a high-end restaurant in downtown Dallas called Town and Country. My father climbed telephone poles and repaired cables for the city. My grandmother worked at a men's tailor shop making buttonholes. During the day my sister was always left down the street with a babysitter, while I remained home with the elderly lady who rented the front bedroom from my grandmother. I called her Mama Helen. She was in her late seventies, slightly handicapped, and needed help to get around. At age four, this became *my* job. I was basically an underage home health aide. Mama Helen taught me how to play Solitaire and we would pass the day while playing cards and listening to soap operas on the radio—*The Guiding Light, Romance of Helen Trent*, and, of course, *Young Dr. Malone*. How Mama Helen got to Texas was a mystery to me, but I knew she came from Pennsylvania and other than us had no family.

My mother worked a split shift and sometimes would come home during her break to put me down for a nap. I could never sleep, never nap—the thought of her leaving again for her shift and not returning until late was too dreadful. I knew my father would be home before her, and he'd be drinking. I would be in for a night of hearing him rant at my poor grandmother who he was thoroughly contemptuous of, mostly because she was Italian and spoke only broken English. Although this turmoil caused by my father frightened me, I would still be comforted to see my grandmother round the corner, walking toward home from the bus stop after work.

Valley Texas Gal

My grandmother kept a chicken coop in the backyard. Many evenings after work she would go out there, grab a chicken and with an axe, expertly dispatch its little chicken soul off to heaven. This was disturbing to me as a small child; I felt sorry for the chicken. But I was torn because my grandmother was an excellent cook! Sometimes my job was to feed the chickens. Many of them were vicious and would try to attack me, especially the rooster who would peck at my legs as I ran for the gate. I felt that the chickens knew their ultimate fate. They would tell me this with their chicken eyes! Chickens are not dumb. A lot of the time I would open the gate, throw all the chicken feed in at once and shut it before the rooster got ahold of me. I suppose he was just doing his job, too. When I was seven, my grandmother made me a sweet little dress out of a chicken feed sack and I loved it.

In 1951, when I was still four, my grandmother made a purchase that would change my life. She bought a small black-and-white television set. I remember it being delivered and perched on top of a table next to the radio. From that moment on, Mama Helen and I watched anything and everything: *Ding Dong School, Search for Tomorrow, Arthur Godfrey Time.* I loved it all! Even the Lucky Strike cigarette commercials. I would mimic, memorize, and reenact. I was swept away into this brand-new world. In the evenings my grandmother and I would watch wrestling together. She was in love with Gorgeous George! Me, not so much, but I was mesmerized by the *golden* bobby pins he would toss out ceremoniously to his adoring fans.

When my father was sober, he too loved watching TV. He would sometimes call out to me saying, "Come in here, Cindy, you're going to like this." It was always something great like *Your Show of Shows, The Milton Berle Show, Jackie Gleason.* When he was sober, he was so much fun. We would laugh out loud at the same things at the same time. When he was sober he was a good father. When he was sober.

I was six when we moved to a small house in Irving, a town about thirteen miles northwest of Dallas. My father bought the house with an acre and a half of land so he could raise pigs and chickens, and harvest the pecans from the huge tree that sat on the property. At that time, Irving was extremely rural, with lots of dirt roads, empty fields, and pastures. I played barefoot and wandered for miles up and down the creek bed alone. I had no fear of the crawdads that nipped at my toes, the spiders and bugs, or the occasional snake crossing the road as the sun went down.

In Texas in those days, kindergarten didn't exist. You started the first grade at the age of six. In September 1953 my mother took me for my first day of school at East Elementary in Irving, Texas. I clung to her and began crying when she tried to leave me. She did her best to reassure me, which made me cling even harder. Mrs. Smith, my teacher, attempted to soothe me, telling me that my mother would be back to pick me up. I knew this wasn't true. She would be working. After she left, I wouldn't see her until the next morning. It was my father who would pick me up and he would most likely be drinking—a secret I could not share with my mother and certainly not with Mrs. Smith.

We were standing on the school playground. My mother pointed out the large slide, and asked me if I wanted to climb up and slide down. I did! I had never been on a slide that high. She took me over and stood at the foot of it, ready to catch me as I flew down to the bottom. I loved it! I climbed back up and slid down two more times with my mother catching me. Holding me, she asked if I would be all right now. I said I would if I could keep

Valley Texas Gal

playing on the slide. Mrs. Smith said, "Yes," for as long as I liked. My mother left and I kept sliding, exhilarated by the speed, forgetting for a while my mother's absence.

My mother had a strict rule about the clothes she bought me and my sister, Carol. No matter what the article of clothing was, it had to be purchased two sizes larger than necessary. This was so we could "grow into them." Oh, and no white clothes, *never* any white clothes. They would only "show the dirt."

By third grade I was either walking home or taking the school bus. The bus driver had a fun rule. The first kid on the bus got to stand by the driver and operate the handle for the door, opening and closing it for each student getting off. Every kid vied for this job, including me. One winter day it was mine! Climbing on the bus first, the bus driver smiled and gestured for me to stand beside him and be the "keeper of the handle." There was one little problem; the brown winter coat my mother bought me was her required two sizes too big. The sleeves hung down, covering my hands like oven mitts. I tried to roll them up, at least to uncover one hand to maneuver the handle. Kids streamed past me to take their seats for the ride home while I struggled with my coat sleeve. When the bus driver was ready to take off, he looked at me and asked, "Ready?"

I had not been able to roll the coat sleeve up far enough so I used it as a glove over the handle and managed to close the door. The driver couldn't help himself; his smile turned into a laugh. I turned around to face the student passengers, who also began to laugh. It was then I got the full measure of what I must look like; sleeves hanging down to my knees; coat to the ground. My mother had purchased a real clown suit! Her system of planning for the future was not working out well for me. I didn't cry. I was, however, humiliated. I looked at the driver and told him I no longer wanted to be the keeper of the handle, and took the closest seat I could find. Like a vampire when the sun goes down, some ambitious kid jumped up and claimed my job. I had no way of knowing at that moment that my mother's practicality would one day work in my favor as I would remember and use this frugal sense of fashion as the basis for the wardrobe of Shirley Wilhelmina Feeney.

My mother was still working at Town and Country and was always gone. She convinced my father that my two-year-old sister should stay with my grandmother in Dallas, leaving me alone when I got home from school. My mother had instructed me to always stay in the house until Daddy got home. And if a tornado was threatening the area, she told me to run to the neighbor's house for shelter in their basement. What my mother didn't know was that if I heard my father's truck pulling up to the house two minutes late, it would mean that he had stopped off for a bottle of Thunderbird. It would also mean that I would likely be spending the night sitting in the locked cab of his truck, parked outside a bar watching a neon Schlitz or Pabst sign blink on and off. I'd sit there waiting for him to stop drinking in the hopes that we would get home in one piece before my mother returned at 11:30 p.m. My father warned me never to tell her.

I always prayed we'd get home without getting into an accident. I would never sleep until my mother came in. I couldn't. I would lay in bed, listening to my father stumbling around in the living room, hoping he wouldn't pass out and start a fire with one of his ever-burning cigarettes. The relief I would feel when my mother finally appeared in my bedroom was euphoric. I could smell the wonderful aroma of fancy restaurant food mixed with her perfume as she bent over to straighten my covers and kiss me goodnight. I would pretend to be asleep, the night out with my father a frightening secret I would keep. These nights continued with my mother being none the wiser. We would sometimes take off and travel as far as Lubbock, so he could drink with his cousins and crazy Aunt Rennie. She would sit me down in the kitchen and preach hellfire and damnation with an ever-present drunken slur. When her sermon was finished, I would be rewarded for my attention with a piece of peanut butter pie. On our ride home every night from wherever our drunken adventures had taken us, if I spoke it would be in soft, quiet tones trying to keep his rage at bay so we could make it back to the house in one piece. Because of these nights of distraction I did not do well in school. I was always sleepy and couldn't concentrate.

On Sundays, my father would waylay his drinking until the afternoon. In the morning he would, without fail, drop me off at church to attend Sunday school. I learned all of my Bible stories. I loved the powerful images and escaped into them. Jesus and Moses and the great people of the Bible. I believed in Jesus and all the miracles, and for that hour in Sunday school, I was safe. I attended many churches—Church of Christ, Baptist Church, Presbyterian Church, United Church of Christ, and Calvary Church. I attended them all! At one point my father even allowed my grandmother to start taking me to the Roman Catholic Church in Dallas where we heard the Mass in Latin. If it was Sunday, I was in church. I even won a Bible for perfect attendance at a tent revival. This was my first stage appearance so I remember it well.

When the preacher called me up to accept my Bible, I was terrified.

"Cynthia, would you like to say a few words to the congregation?" He held the microphone to my mouth.

Trembling, I could only manage one word. "No!" I was presented my Bible and traveled back down the aisle, people reaching out to pat me on the head.

I was ten when my mother and father announced we were moving back to California. My grandmother would be going with us. Her brother, Joe, had moved with his family to California two years previously and opened a shoe repair store. By then Mama Helen had passed away. The only ones attending her funeral were my grandmother, my mother, my father, my sister, and me.

We drove cross-country caravan style. Naturally, I rode with my father in the truck while my mother, sister, and grandmother followed us in a '56 Chevy. The trip turned out to be an unexpected pleasure because my father stayed sober the entire way. At first we lived in an apartment in Santa Monica. It was damp and cold compared to the heat we had "battled" in Texas, as my mother would say. In a month my parents found a small house back in The Valley to buy. My mother immediately got a job working at a restaurant at the Van Nuys airport. My father was hired at an electronic manufacturing company, and my grandmother retired to the back bedroom in the new little house, where she returned to watching her soap operas and wrestling matches. We lived in a traditional American neighborhood with friendly people and orderly sidewalks lined with plum trees. I loved it except that my mother continued to opt for a nighttime shift at the restaurant, which allowed my father free rein to resume his all-night drinking. This was my normal.

We had a fenced-in backyard and a large garage. Here I began putting on shows, writing and directing sketches, enlisting my sister to costar with me. We packed them in! Neighbor kids came in droves, sometimes bringing their dogs. Everyone sat on old chairs and trunks that I had fashioned into makeshift stadium seating. We became a big hit in the neighborhood! Around this same time, my mother and father found a new church for me and my sister, Carol, to attend—the First Methodist Church of Reseda. I joined the Methodist Youth Fellowship. The MYF, among other things, helped to sponsor the church's ice-cream social. This particular year, they wanted to put on a talent show. With the vast experience I had garnered from our stupendous garage productions, I volunteered. I poured my soul into the show—writing, casting, directing, and, of course, acting. I wrote a Soupy Sales parody, which was a real crowd-pleaser. We sold out both performances at fifty cents a ticket. When church camp rolled around, they asked me to help out with that talent show, too. It was so encouraging.

High school was a game-changer for me. First of all, I made a great friend—Lorie Gorenbein. She was very bright, with a wicked sense of humor. We were each other's confidante, as girls will be. She was strong in ways I was weak and vice versa. We each had mothers who were strict about our sugar intake and eating habits, but in different ways. Where my mother's kitchen was stocked with Brewer's yeast, alfalfa sprouts, unpasteurized milk, and bran, Lorie's mother, Natalie, kept her refrigerator filled with actual edible foods like bagels and cream cheese. What neither of them knew was that we would sneak off on Saturdays and go to the local McDonald's. We'd each buy a bagful of twenty-two-cent cheeseburgers and twelve-cent fries. Then we'd mosey over to June Ellen's Doughnuts, which was right across from the high school, and buy three doughnuts each! Then we'd swing by the Orange Julius for a beverage. We'd take it all back to her house, hide in her bedroom, and eat really fast, praying we wouldn't get caught. My sister once warned us to watch out, because one day we'd wake up and be blimps! But that junk food was no match for our teenage metabolisms.

Lorie and I were involved in high school politics. I was voted in as the Girls' League director of publicity and she was voted in as the Girls' League activities director. Girls' League was a school organization that handled functions such as dances, homecoming, fundraisers, and dress board. Female students who had been ticketed for dress-code violations such as skirt above the knees, improper grooming, or inappropriate hairstyle (too much ratting) were called before the dress board. These girls would then be chastised for heinous fashion infractions that if left unchecked would surely lead to a life of crime and degradation. For some reason, as Girls' League director of publicity, I had the dubious honor of conducting this crucible. Anyone with three tickets was automatically suspended. One of my jobs was also to collect the tickets and deposit them in a box in the Girls' vice principal's office for her to review.

These "tainted" girls were instructed to come to the auditorium at lunchtime on Wednesdays and stand before the board for questioning. The first time I conducted this meeting I was upset to see some members of the board eating their lunch while our quarry stood before us. I thought it was rude and asked them to stop. Some became indignant and wanted to know just when they were supposed to have their lunch. I said I didn't care, as long as it wasn't until after we finished with dress board. I must confess I didn't really care about eating my lunch, since my mother had recently discovered alfalfa sprouts and was now including large handfuls in my warm and wet tuna salad sandwiches.

See, here's the thing. Each week the same girls were called in. Girls who didn't come from a family that had the kind of money to afford matching sweater-sets. They came from homes filled with financial and emotional strife, or worse. You could see it in the way they cast their eyes down in embarrassment and humiliation, or clinched their thumb in the palm of their hand for something to hold onto. This group of girls just couldn't see past their own lunch to observe the trauma they were inflicting. My friend Lorie felt the same way, and this is why instead of taking over the tickets to the Girls' vice principal's office, we deep-sixed them in a trash can behind the auditorium. But the thought did cross my mind about getting caught or called into the vice principal's office to be asked why she hadn't received any tickets.

Lorie even said, "Cin, what if we get caught?"

I told her, "If that time ever comes, we'll think of something."

We didn't have to wait long. That time came swiftly one day, marching down the hall behind us.

"Miss Gorenbien! Miss Williams!" It was the dreaded Girls' vice principal.

"I need to speak with both of you!"

Lorie and I could not slow down. We could not allow her to catch up with us until we rearranged our skirts to fall below our knees. We did this by unrolling them at the waistband. We made it by the skin of our teeth before she swept in.

Putting an arm around each of our shoulders and squeezing tight, she said, "Girls! I've been meaning to call you into the office." Even with the Girls' vice principal between us, I could practically hear Lorie's heart pounding. "I have to let you both know how proud I am of the work the Girls' League has been doing this semester. Our dress code campaign has paid off! I haven't received one violation ticket. Good work!"

Shirley, I Jest!

We sputtered out our thank-yous as she traveled on down the hall. That night we went to McDonald's and Orange Julius celebrate. (June Ellen's Donuts was closed.)

Along with Girls' League, I tried out for many school activities. The swim team—didn't make it. The cheerleading squad—didn't make it. But then one illustrious day, auditions were held for the school talent show, so I tried out by performing a Bob Newhart routine, "The Driving Instructor." Not only did I make it into the talent show, but the drama teacher, Mr. Kulp, asked me to take Play Production. He said if I had an elective open, he would skip me past Drama I and put me into Drama II and Play Production. (Thank you, Bob Newhart!) The Play Production class was filled with people who were different from the rest of the student body. There was a kind of electric camaraderie. We performed *Our Town*, *The Man Who Came to Dinner*, *The Bald Soprano*, *The Madwoman of Chaillot*, and *The Diary of Anne Frank*. Mr. Kulp was a formidable director who expected discipline and excellence.

In the class was a girl named Sally Field. I was in awe of her. Even at fifteen she was a great actress. When we would perform plays, she would be in the "A" cast. I would be in the "B" cast. She was head cheerleader. I had sprained my ankle on the down-beat of my routine. I did, however, make it to the drill team. She soon left school to play *Gidget* and then *The Flying Nun*. Sally was going to be on television. How exciting! For as much as I loved acting, I didn't dare consider it as a potential career. So I started thinking about becoming a registered nurse. More specifically, an ER nurse. I loved the idea of helping people in crisis, tending to them, comforting and reassuring them. Not to mention the drama of the PA system calling "Nurse Williams, you're wanted in Emergency." There were two small problems. One, I could only manage

Valley Texas Gal

to get a C in Mrs. Katzman's physiology class and that was after repeating it in summer school. Who would want to be tended to by a nurse with a C in physiology? And the second problem was blood! When I saw it, I passed out! My nursing career became a fading dream.

My grandmother had been suffering from heart problems, and one day took a turn for the worse and was rushed to the hospital where she passed away. When my mother came home early the next morning and broke the news to us, I asked her if Grandma had suffered. She said, "It was the strangest thing. I woke up in the night and found her awake, praying. I could tell she was weak. I asked her 'Mama, are you afraid?' She had a big smile on her face, her eyes were bright and clear like a twelve-year-old and she said 'No, Frances, I'm not afraid' and a few minutes later she was gone. Oh, Cindy, it was peaceful! I hope I go that way."

And even at the age of sixteen, I thought "Me too!"

By the time high school graduation rolled around, I knew I had no chance of scoring high enough on the SAT to get into a university. And even if I had, I knew I would never be able to afford it unless I got a scholarship. With my grade average being a C+ that was never going to be the case. In the end, fate drove me. I found the Los Angeles City College Theatre Arts Department. Friends in my high school drama class had mentioned it, and a few were going to enroll. And that's what I decided to do, too. My father was absolutely against it. He did not want me to move out of the house. My mother tried to talk me into taking a secretarial course. Even if I had decided to do this instead, I knew it would be futile because I had taken typing in high school and could do no better than thirty-two words a minute with three mistakes. No, I had no future and no business being a secretary. My mother finally relented and they paid the minimum enrollment fees, plus $40 monthly rent for a room in a house across the street from the college, and $10 a week living expenses. I had very little money and no car, but still I was thrilled to be out of the house and enrolled in Theatre Arts.

On the first day of college, those enrolled in the Theatre Arts department were gathered for orientation. Jerry Blunt, head of the department, addressed us. He told us that out of the 308 enrolled for the two-and-a-half-year program, only twelve would make it through to the end. That's how serious this theater arts program was. I was excited about the challenge. I looked around the assembly hall wondering who these twelve people would be, and hoped I stood a chance.

We hit the ground running. The required courses were Beginning Acting with a scene prepared each week. We had to take Costuming or Shop. I chose Costuming. A Dialect class, a History of the World Theatre class, and Stage Movement were all required. We had to maintain excellence and discipline. Three tardy marks and we were out of the program. It was rigorous. But I loved every single moment of it. I had found my niche; I was like a duck to water. I was exhausted and inspired all at the same time.

In my Beginning Acting class I met a fellow student named Lynne Stewart. She was so talented and had a phenomenal sense of humor. We were partners on our first scene assignment and had to write and perform a three-minute pantomime. Lynne and I wrote about two women sitting on a park bench, sharing a box of popcorn, people watching, then getting very competitive over a handsome guy walking by. We got an A! We also got a few laughs! Lynne and I became best friends and have been ever since. She would go on to play Miss Yvonne on *Pee Wee's Playhouse*, and

Valley Texas Gal

years later we would marvel over the fact that dolls had been made in the likeness of the characters we had played—Miss Yvonne and Shirley Feeney.

When it came time to buy books for courses, I had to ask my mother for the money. My mother could not grasp this concept.

"Why is there a charge for schoolbooks? Schoolbooks are given out freely by the school."

I tried to explain that it is different in college; you have to buy your own books. My mother's response was, "Well then, you're going to have to get a job and pay for your books yourself, because I don't have any more money to give you."

I went to the Financial Aid office to apply for a small loan, but was turned down because ironically my parents' combined income was a little too much for me to qualify. So I did as my mother said and got a job working in downtown Los Angeles. I had to leave school after my eleven o'clock class each day to catch the bus to Union Street where I worked for a law firm as a relief PBX operator. When the receptionist took lunch, I worked the switchboard. Also part of my job was closing files of cases that the firm had completed. I was good at the PBX part but lost when it came to closing what were referred to as "dead files." I would do some artful maneuvering on my desk so that the stack of files would appear to have dwindled. (They were in my bottom desk drawer!) I told myself I'd get to them tomorrow. (I felt very guilty.) I managed to keep this job through the first semester. However, because of bus fare and other expenses I hadn't counted on, I was never able to save enough money to buy my books. When I needed to study from a particular textbook, I would borrow them from Lynne. If I needed to study for a play, I checked them out of the campus library. And I managed. I was never late for class. I always had my scene work prepared, and by the second semester I started a new job near the school at the International House of Pancakes on Vermont and Santa Monica.

In the Theatre Arts program you had to finish a year maintaining good grades before you were eligible to be cast in one of the productions. The teachers would watch you carefully in your acting class and in T.A.4, a class that was open to the entire student body. It was held in the main theater and once a week the best scenes from all the acting classes would be presented before this audience while teachers took notes for casting possibilities for the plays they were going to direct. Lynne and I were selected with a scene from *Waiting for Godot*. This time we got a triple A!

There was another actor at City College who also became my friend. His name was Vern Joyce. Vern was breathtaking on stage. The entire Theatre Arts department was in awe of him, including the entire faculty. He could play anything. From Puck in *A Midsummer Night's Dream* to Willy Loman in *Death of a Salesman*. A testimony to his greatness is that years later when he had auditioned for the Actors Studio and made it through all the rounds and down to his final audition, he asked me if I would be his scene partner. I was thrilled! I always wanted to work with Vern. We chose a scene from *Petulia*, a movie that starred George C. Scott and Julie Christie.

The scene could *only* be three minutes long, and that included entering and setting the furniture and props, using what was already available on stage. Lee Strasberg himself would be one of the three judges watching in the darkness. We had rehearsed long and hard and the scene was excellent. I was only slightly nervous because it wasn't my audition; it was Vern's. Vern had explained to me that no matter where we were in the scene after three minutes, they would say "thank you." We would stop, say "thank you," and exit. And that's how it went.

A month later I got a call from a friend who was a member of the Actors Studio. He told me they had posted the names of the new members. There were nine of them. Not only had Vern made the cut, but they had made me a member also. Robert De Niro and Sally Field were also among the nine. I have my Actors Studio card and that honor is one of the greatest in my life, and a great big nod to the talent and brilliance of my friend, Vern.

By the summer of 1968 I finished my courses at LACC. Mr. Blunt was almost right—the class I began with had dwindled down to thirteen students instead of twelve! I was proud I had made it, and have always thought of myself as the thirteenth student. I stopped working at the International House of Pancakes and moved in with some friends to an enormous old mansion on Los Feliz in Hollywood. It had once belonged to W. C. Fields. I took the "maid's room," which was already furnished with a comfortable mattress on the floor. My needs were simple at this point in my life. With four of us sharing the rent, I needed to get another job immediately. I found one on Wilshire Boulevard, once again, waiting tables in a restaurant called Ye Piccadilly Deli.

At this time I had no car so I would walk up to Hollywood Boulevard to catch the bus to and from work. I liked this job! The owners were very nice. They introduced me to Dr. Brown's Cream Soda. I had a good time working there—for two weeks! Then, one of my friends told me they were hiring cocktail waitresses at the Whisky a Go Go on the Sunset Strip, and I should call to apply. I knew I had a good job, but this would be a *great* job, working around live music and fascinating people. I called. I was given a brief interview over the phone and asked to come down to the club that day. I met with Mario Maglieri, one of the owners of the Whisky. He asked to see my driver's license to make sure I was twenty-one, since I would be serving cocktails. He hired me on the spot. Mario told me that I was to show up at 4 p.m. the next day for training. I asked him about uniforms. He said they didn't have uniforms. The girls wore their own clothes. He looked me over and added, "Like what you've got on is OK, I guess."

"What I've got on?" I thought.

I was wearing the only skirt I owned, a beige wraparound, with an ill-fitting white blouse and cheap, shiny black pumps. That was as far as my wardrobe went unless you counted a pair of worn-out bell-bottom jeans, a couple of pullover tops, moccasins, and some love beads! I had hoped for some sort of uniform, a black apron or a T-shirt perhaps, with the club logo on it. At the House of Pancakes, we had bright orange outfits, stiff white aprons, and little white hats plus sensible shoes. Somehow I would have to make it work, because I wanted this job.

I left the club elated and headed straight to a payphone. I now had the difficult task of quitting my job at Ye Piccadilly Deli. I stood at the phone for a few minutes thinking of what to say. I felt bad. It was like leaving a childhood sweetheart for the lead singer in a rock-and-roll band. I took a breath and dialed. The manager answered.

"Hi, it's Cindy," I said.

"Hi, Cindy."

Get it over with, I thought.

"I'm sorry but I have to quit."

Silence.

"What? You have to quit? Why?"

"I had an accident. I broke my arm."

Silence.

"No, you didn't."

"Yes, yes I did. I'm so sorry. I know you'll have to hire someone else and I understand."

"How'd you break it?"

"Bus accident."

Silence.

"A bus *hit* you?"

"No, I fell getting off the bus."

"No, you didn't."

Dead silence.

"I did!"

Awkward silence.

"OK, Cindy, but I know it's not true."

Hideous silence.

"OK."

"Bye, Cindy."

"Bye."

I felt so bad, I'd disappointed these nice people and to boot I was a horrible liar. Good at the concoction, but not at the execution. I vowed *never* to lie again.

(A little lie I told myself.)

TWO

Love, Peace, and Happiness

In 1968 the Sunset Strip was a wonderland of music, neon lights, love, peace, and happiness. A magical place, and I had just landed a magical job there, waiting tables at the Whisky a Go Go.

It's my first night and Chicago Transit Authority is the headliner with the Flying Burrito Brothers opening for them. I can hardly believe my good luck—working around live music! The day before, a girl named Maggie and I were trained by one of the seasoned waitresses. Among other things she showed us how to hold the tray; shoulder high, palm up, fingers back. This way you had a natural swivel when you brought the tray around to serve. (While I worked there, my hand tended to stay in this position even when I slept.) We were given a tour. The go-go cages had been taken down two months earlier. I was a little disappointed, I have to admit.

The stage at the Whisky was elevated above the dance floor. On stage, to the far right, was a ramp that performers took to travel on and off stage. If you followed the ramp from the stage and kept going, it would end up backstage where the dressing rooms were. That meant whoever worked the upstairs bar also worked the backstage area. Those girls would serve all members of the bands, plus friends and family. The upstairs was referred to as "The Peanut Gallery" because along with a bar, a small dance floor, and a couple of tables, it consisted mainly of benches similar to bleacher seating. People in the Peanut Gallery were exempt from the standard two-drink minimum, which was imposed in the downstairs area. Kids would head upstairs right away because they knew they could pay the cover charge and get an inexpensive drink to last all night while they listened to incredible music. No one ever tipped up there, and I Do Mean No One!

To compensate, Mario would always give whoever worked it ten dollars at the end of the night. Most nights before the club opened, as we prepared our trays and lit the red candles on the round tables, Mario would, cigar in-hand, give a little speech regarding the acts, reminding us to enforce the two-drink minimum, and any other tidbit he thought we might need to know. On my first night I've been given the VIP section in front of the red leather booths. How lucky could I get? The slide show was beginning with random images of current events, Richard Nixon, Russia, hippies protesting, love-ins. Psychedelic images are underscored by the fabulous music of the day: The Beatles, The Rolling Stones, Buffalo Springfield, Simon and Garfunkel, Jimi Hendrix, Eric Burdon and the Animals. The doors opened and people flooded into the club. Suddenly I see people sitting at a table in my section. I happily approach, noting three pretty blond girls and a long-haired man sitting with his back to me. I greet them saying, "Hi, what can I get you?"

Each blond girl says, in turn, "Tom Collins, Tom Collins, Tom Collins," and I write it down.

Love, Peace, and Happiness

"Tom Collins, Tom Collins, Tom Collins." I turn to the guy who still has his back to me and ask him the same question.

"What can I get you to drink, sir?"

He turns to face me for the first time and that's when Jim Morrison asks me to bring him a bottle of Jack Daniels to the table. I was stunned by how beautiful he was; everything about him glistened. He took my breath away but I pretended not to notice it was him. After all, I had been a drama major and was trained in the art of pretending. I wrote down "bottle of Jack" and hustled off to the bar to put in my ticket.

As I started to leave, Tony the bartender shouted at me, "Hey new girl, wait a minute." He was calling me back.

"What the hell is this?" he asks me holding up the ticket. "Three Tom Collins and a bottle of Jack? Is Morrison in the club?" he asked.

I ran back to him trying to conceal my excitement. "Yes, Jim Morrison's in the club! The bottle of Jack is for him."

Tony looked at me and said, "You know perfectly well we can't serve a bottle of Jack at the table." Well, I didn't know perfectly well we couldn't serve a bottle of Jack at the table. Someone must have left that part out when they trained me. Then Tony says, "You go back there and tell him, I'll pour him a single or a double but no bottle of Jack at the table." I hesitate.

"Go!" he says and I hustle back toward my table with the three blondes and Jim. I notice that the customers at my other table— two tall black gentlemen, one wearing a purple suit; both wearing big hats, and their nicely dressed dates are staring at me. I give them a smile and scurry past them.

I get back to Jim's table and deliver the message, "I'm sorry, Mr. Morrison, but I'm not allowed to serve a bottle of Jack at the table. I can bring you a single or a double."

Shirley, I Jest!

He looks at me and asks, "Is Tony tending bar tonight?"

"Yes, he is," I answer.

"Well, you go back there and tell Tony that he's served me a bottle of Jack at the table before and I want a bottle of Jack at the table tonight."

I turn tail and rush back to Tony. The Flying Burrito Brothers are playing "Do Right Woman." My shoes are killing me!

Tony's waiting for me.

"Spare me the sob story, what's he asking for now?"

"Same thing. He says you've served him a bottle of Jack at the table and he wants one tonight!"

"That son-of-a-bitching liar! You go back there and tell him he's a liar, and he's not getting a bottle of Jack at the table and that's that!"

"I can't call Jim Morrison a liar!"

"Go!" he says.

I jump. I head back, ignoring the big-hat table still beckoning me. The second I get to the table, Jim looks up.

"I am so sorry, Mr. Morrison. It seems I'm really not allowed to serve a bottle of Jack at the table. Would a couple of doubles do?"

"Not really. Do me a favor, go back there and you insist for me!"

I'm kind of upset now, and my feet are really starting to hurt from my cheap shoes. I say the only thing I can think of, "OK!"

I head back to Tony determined this time to get that bottle of Jack for Jim. As I approach, I see that the blond girls' Tom Collins drinks are sitting on the bar. I quickly put them on my tray. Tony looks at me but before he can speak I say, "He wants his bottle of Jack and he means it!"

Love, Peace, and Happiness

And then I take off before Tony has a chance to torture me with his bartending manifesto. As I'm going back to Jim's table, the two black guys make eye contact with me. They want to know when I'm going to be over there, I give them a nod as if to say "be right with you." I get back to Jim's table and gingerly place a Tom Collins in front of each of the girls. He looks at me as if to ask, When? Bottle? Jack?

I say as calmly as I can, "I'm working on it."

The Flying Burrito Brothers have ratcheted up the music. If only I could enjoy it. If only I could enjoy anything about my first night waiting tables at the fabulous Whisky a Go Go, which right now is not so fabulous. Gypsy Boots, an actor and alternative lifestyle guru, has taken to the dance floor with his dancers (girls who looked to be around the age of fourteen, dressed in chiffon and gauze with flowers in their hair). Music swirls around me in the club as I make my way to the "big hat" table, wishing for the good old days, back at the International House of Pancakes (home of the bottomless coffeepot).

"What can I get you?"

The two women look at me and each say in turn, "Tom Collins."

Hmm, I'm seeing a trend here. Ladies like their Tom Collins. I wondered what was in them. I turn to the men and they look at me and each order a Zombie. Now a Zombie is a drink with triple liquor and while I was being schooled the day before, I was informed we had to charge double for them. I take their order and head back to Tony who is waiting for me in the sixth ring of hell. I put my new order up on the bar. Tony glances at it.

"Zombies, ha-ha, I *like* to mix Zombies! Make sure you charge them double. What about Morrison?"

I look him straight in the eye as boldly as I can and I say these words: "Bottle of Jack." I can practically see smoke coming out of his nostrils.

"You go back there and tell that fucker I'll have the bouncer throw his ass out of here! I don't care *who* he is!"

"You jerk!" I think, as I start to cry and stumble my way back to Jim's table for possibly the last time. I hear Jim singing "The End" in my head.

"I'm *so* sorry Mr. Morrison, but I really can't bring that bottle of Jack to the table. Can *I* buy you your double?"

Jim Morrison responds by taking my hand and looking me in the eyes, "What's your name?"

"Cindy."

He gently says, "Well, Miss Cindy, bring me that double. We've just been playing with ya!"

I look around and see all the waitresses, plus Mario and Tony, laughing at me. Could it be? Could it be a practical joke? Has Jim Morrison played a practical joke on me? I felt honored and humiliated both at the same time. I realize that Jim is still holding my hand. He squeezes it and smiles at me. I smile back. I'm too weak to squeeze his hand. I stand there a moment, letting the adrenaline subside. And now I can really feel my damn cheap pumps pinching my feet. I reluctantly let go of Jim's hand and trot off to the bar where Tony ruffles my hair and laughs. I see that my Zombies and the other Tom Collins drinks are ready to go. I put them on my tray, take a deep breath, and head off. I set the Tom Collins down in front of the girls and the Zombies in front of each of the men. As I start to walk off, one of the men taps my arm. I turn around.

He looks at me and says, "Light 'em!"

"Light 'em?"

Love, Peace, and Happiness

"Yeah, light 'em. If these drinks have triple the liquor, they'll catch afire!"

I had not been trained in this customer request either. But if he wants his drink lit, I'll give it the old junior college try! I set my tray down and grab one of the official Whisky matchbooks off the table and, inwardly trembling, do as the gentlemen requested. I light his drink afire, holding the match over the Zombie.

Boom! It goes up in a majestic blue flame, as does the other one. *Whoosh*! I'm thinking, "Bravo, Tony."

They smile at me, but not in a Jim Morrison way. I retreat from the table back to the bar. Tony is waiting for me. He says, "Those guys actually thought we had cut them short with the drinks, but I love mixing Zombies."

"Yes," I said. "But you should have warned me about the fire thing!"

The Flying Burrito Brothers have left the stage and now, "Sympathy for the Devil" is blasting out over the club speakers with the light show going full-bore. Gypsy Boots sways and circles one of his little girl dancers and others join in. Good God, you could see right through the gossamer! They circle each other with liquid arm movements—hands and fingertips moving in front of their eyes, bodies swaying in some sort of slow-motion whirling dervish. I thought, "This is the kind of dancing you might witness if you had lived a past life in Atlantis!"

I was always fascinated by this and years later would mimic these moves in a funny dance we did on *Laverne & Shirley*.

I checked on Jim's table, and he was gone! They were all gone! One of the waitresses said, "Don't worry about the check. The club took care of it."

Shirley, I Jest!

What about the tip? Did Jim leave me a tip or maybe a note? I wanted to ask this, but I didn't dare. Besides it really didn't matter. The experience with him was more important than any tip. But still! I scurried to my Zombie table and asked if everyone was doing OK. Lo and behold they were, and now they wanted Zombies all around plus cheeseburgers and fries. I wrote down the new order. I started to make my way back to the bar to put in my order when Maggie, the other new waitress, came to me crying.

"What's the matter?" I asked.

She said she had tripped and spilled her tray, then she had messed up an order, and now she was being sent upstairs to the dreaded Peanut Gallery.

"Poor Maggie," I thought, but then maybe it was for the best. After all, downstairs was just too challenging for some people, and I couldn't help but think that with all of my waitressing experience it came as second nature to me. A thrilling blast of horns rang out. Chicago Transit Authority had taken the stage!

The next night *I* was relegated to the Peanut Gallery, where they had intended me to work in the first place. I didn't really mind, I was still kind of flattered by the whole Jim Morrison thing. I kept my job at the Whisky for another two months, serving everyone from Duke Ellington to Joe Cocker. I could tell many fantastic tales about working the Peanut Gallery at the Whisky, and maybe one day I will.

THREE

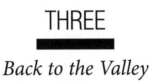

Back to the Valley

I had to quit the Whisky because I couldn't support myself on what I made working upstairs in the land of low tips. After that job, I was back in my old orange uniform working the graveyard shift at the International House of Pancakes, this time on Sunset Boulevard. I had managed to buy an old car for ninety dollars. It probably only had eight or nine rides left in it! When it did conk out, I had to leave IHOP because it was too difficult to take the bus. Eventually everyone moved out of the group house on Los Feliz.

I started sharing a basement apartment on Glendale Boulevard in Echo Park with Edna, a good friend from college. Money, of course, was still an issue, mainly because neither Edna nor I had any! Edna got a job in Hollywood (tearing taped dimes off sweepstakes entries). I reregistered with the same employment agency that had placed me with the law firm.

Within a week, I landed a job at a bank in downtown L.A. Initially I was to be trained as a teller, but first they had another little task for me. I was put in a big room with massive fluorescent lighting. They brought in several boxes. These boxes were filled

Shirley, I Jest!

with two thousand 2 × 4 index cards. On each card was the name and information of one of the bank's customers. Each of these customers had applied for a newfangled thing called a "charge card." My mission was to alphabetize the cards and then run credit checks. Depending on their score I was then to issue them the appropriate credit amount. It felt like a lot of responsibility for me to extend credit to these customers. I learned two things about myself at the bank. One, I am a great alphabetizer and, two, refer to number one. I organized the names, in order, in three days, no problem. But calling to check out a person's financial statistics and then to determine if they were a good credit risk would, even under incandescent lighting, be *vile*! I felt like I was searching through their underwear drawers looking for a gun that had been used in a crime!

Who in their right mind would put *me* in charge of such a task? I'll tell you who—the very nice, and very handsome bank manager who hired me. The employment agency must have done some fancy footwork. Maybe they told him about the job I'd had at the law firm and that convinced him I was bank teller material. He had no way of knowing about the "dead files" in the *bottom* drawer! And here's the kicker. I was solely in charge of this task and "the people in the boxes." I alone had to determine the limit on the card according to the calculated score. I was in charge of the applications and could check off whatever limit I deemed appropriate, up to one thousand dollars.

I spent my precious breaks sampling the vending machine fare while mulling this over, absentmindedly eating candy, chips, cookies and more candy and drinking coffee. I started empathizing with these people and began toying around with the idea of issuing most of them the thousand dollar limit even if they didn't meet the criteria. I thought of the elderly people in those boxes in the same way I thought of my grandmother: honest, hardworking, always paying her debts, and perhaps needing a break more than others. But then, what if they defaulted? All of them? Oh, and were sent to prison! And somehow I was linked to it, then arrested, tried, convicted, and put in the same prison where my elderly people had now formed a gang and tormented me on a daily basis? I was consuming way too much candy!

One day while sitting in my "office" in another caffeine-sugar daze, the door swung open. The handsome bank manager asked me to come with him for a moment. I was hoping at this point that he was going to fire me. But no such luck. He led me to the bank vault. A guard and a female teller were waiting.

"We want to train you to assist with the safety deposit boxes. Don't worry, you'll go back to credit, but we want you to learn this first."

I thought he was kidding, but he wasn't. He was smiling at me with an expression that seemed to exude his total confidence, as if to say, *I believe in you, Cindy.* They were all so nice as they ran me through the drill and handed me a key that was tethered to an official-looking chain. I would be responsible for this key. When customers wished to gain access to their safety deposit box, I would walk with them into the vault. They would insert and turn their key; I would insert and turn the bank's key, simple as that. First time up to bat, I escorted the customer into the vault to his safety deposit box. He inserted his key and turned it. I inserted the bank's key and turned it. It immediately jammed and twisted in the lock. I tried pulling it out. No luck! It wouldn't budge. I had the chain around my neck! It was a little too short for me to take off. The nice bank manager called some sort of security locksmith who would not, as it happened, be available for two hours! I apologized to the customer and the bank manager. I stood there guarding the twisted key, thinking about all *my people* waiting under the fluorescent lights for me to approve their credit. I saw my banking career fading away. And it *did*. Completely!

I was kindly let go. I thought about trying to get my job back at IHOP. I was not going to show my face around the employment agency anymore. Edna still had her job in Hollywood and was doing okay until one Thursday morning when she found out her boyfriend, Kenny, was coming down from San Francisco to see her on Friday. She needed Friday and the weekend off and asked me to call in to work for her and tell them she was ill.

"Ill with what?" I asked.

"I don't know. Something that keeps me out of work till Monday."

"Like what?"

She thought for a moment, and then came up with, "Appendicitis."

"Really? Can't that be serious?" I asked. She thought again.

"Tell them I have to go to the hospital."

I called her boss and told her that Edna was suffering from appendicitis and had to go to the hospital. Her boss, a lovely lady, was sympathetic and asked where the office should send flowers. I was stymied. I looked at Edna. She was standing there but could not hear the other end of the conversation. She gave me a look as if to ask, *What? What's going on?*

I told the boss that flowers wouldn't be necessary. The boss finished by telling me that everyone in the office just loved Edna and they would be thinking of her and praying for a quick recovery. I had a *baaad* feeling! Edna enjoyed a great weekend, and returned to work Monday morning where she was swiftly fired. To this day, any time this story is recalled, Edna and I wince and laugh at our stupidity.

Soon after this, Edna's luck turned around. She was offered a scholarship in a government-sponsored filmmaking workshop called New Communicators. She would be writing and directing her very own film. How exciting! I, on the other hand, caught the flu, which turned into bronchitis and had to return to my parents' house in the Valley so my mother could take care of me.

My mother was so happy to have me home. She could hardly wait to nurse me back to health. She was now working at the juice bar at Jack LaLanne's European Health Spa in Reseda. She loved her job. People enjoyed her effervescent personality and her knowledge of health and preventative medicine.

During the time I was back at home in Reseda, my father was diagnosed with lung cancer. My mother had tried for some time to get him to see a doctor, secretly diagnosing him herself. This was no real surprise; my father had smoked three packs of unfiltered cigarettes every day for as long as I could remember. My mother finally convinced my father to see a doctor. He came home with the awful news. He had a mass on his left lung. He called a Baptist minister who came to the house to council and pray with him. After this he never drank again.

Around the same time Edna called and asked me if I wanted to interview for New Communicators, the filmmaking workshop she was involved with. I jumped at the chance and said "Yes!" She said, "Good!" and took it upon herself to schedule the interview. I wasn't sure if I had the right credentials for the workshop. I was an actress, not a writer or filmmaker, but maybe I could become one and maybe I could write and act in my *own* film.

Shirley, I Jest!

I was nervous walking into the interview, but more than that my feet were killing me from the same cheap shoes I had been wearing since I worked at the Whisky. My nerves subsided when I entered the room. The two program directors couldn't have been nicer. They immediately put me at ease. But after interviewing me, they had to turn me down for two reasons. I didn't fit the criteria for the program because I was an actress, not a filmmaker. The other reason was the program provided artistic opportunities for low-income minorities. (Edna is an African American writer.) Affirmative action had just been put into place, and they rightly were trying to balance the scales that had been so unfair to people of color for so long. I argued that I was a minority myself; I was half Sicilian, and my family was economically challenged.

I was told, "Cindy, you're an actress, that's what you studied to be. We know two young producers who are starting a management company for young talent. We'd love to call them and set up an interview for you. Their names are Garry Marshall and Fred Roos."

A week later I found myself sitting in front of the mirror at my mother's vanity. I was wearing my Whisky wraparound skirt, my ill-fitting white blouse, and those same cheap, crappy black patent leather pumps. I was looking into her magnifying mirror contemplating my eyebrows, which were too thick and too unruly. I was also covering up the chronic dark circles under my eyes, desperate to appear pretty and professional for this important interview.

I glanced out my mother's bedroom door and down the short hallway that separated her bedroom from my father's. I could see him sitting in his chair. He was watching television. I was sad for him. We all were. The cancer had trumped the bad feelings that all of us had held toward him. That afternoon my mother was taking him to the VA to check in for his surgery that was scheduled for the next morning. The surgeons were attempting to remove the mass from his lung and hopefully save him.

He called to me, "Cindy, honey, come here." I got up from the vanity and walked toward his room. "Look at this guy, you're gonna like him." I stepped inside his room, and turned toward the TV. Bob Dylan was singing "Tambourine Man."

I said, "That's Bob Dylan, Daddy. And you're right, I *do* like him!"

"He's real good, I like him a lot. I like the way he sings," he said.

"Me too," I said. I kissed my father and told him I loved him.

As I turned to go, he said, "I love you, too, honey, and good luck with your interview."

I replied, "Good luck to you, too, Daddy."

Someone once said that change is the only constant in life. And both my father's life and my own were about to do just that.

Although my mind was filled with concern for my father, the meeting with Garry Marshall and Fred Roos seemed to be going well. They asked me a little bit about myself. I summed up my entire acting career to that point; which consisted of the plays I had been in at Birmingham High School, and Los Angeles City College. And for good measure I threw in writing, directing, and acting in "The Ice Cream Social Talent Show" for the First Methodist Church of Reseda. If they weren't impressed, they were at least amused, and they seemed to like me. Garry Marshall asked me to get up and turn around. I did. His comment to Fred Roos was, "I like her. She's like a pudgy Barbara Harris." I was thrilled to be compared to this Tony-winning Broadway comic legend. I didn't even mind the "pudgy" part.

I liked both of them, and had to contain my joy when they told me they wanted to represent me in their newly formed company, Compass Management. I left their office in a state of euphoria.

The next morning we learned the surgeons could not remove the mass from my father's lung. The mass had fused both lungs together. It was inoperable. Three days later they sent him home. We didn't have the money to pay for professional help leaving my mother, my sister Carol, and me to tend to him day and night. It was brutal. He had a scar down his chest that went under his rib cage and up his back. My mother dressed his wounds. He was too weak to eat or drink. I would ask him if he wanted me to find a good TV show to watch. He'd say, "No." None of this would matter; he had a high fever and by the time a week had passed the cancer had spread to his brain. He began hallucinating. One morning he yelled for me to pull the fishing hooks out of his legs. The cancer had compromised his entire being. We took him back to the VA, this time for the awful hospice care they offered. I despised the hospital's putrid smell, its colors were drab and sickly. My poor father would die in this horrible place. You would think that for those who fought for America excellent health care would be a given. Instead he suffered an agonizing death on dingy, yellowed sheets. In the end he was released from his demons, as were my mother, my sister, and I.

Years later, I contemplated my father's death, and thought how different I could have cared for him had it come during my success. I would have gotten him the best of care in a beautiful place with nurses tending to him around the clock.

After my father died, my career started to take off. Compass Management arranged an interview for me with the Paul Kohner Agency. They liked me enough in the initial meeting to ask me

Back to the Valley

to come in and perform a three-minute dramatic scene and a three-minute comedy scene. I found a scene partner and we performed in the office at the Kohner Agency with Paul Kohner, Carl Forrest, and the rest of the agents seated around us. The next day they called and wanted to sign me. I was ecstatic! The first audition my new agent got me was for a then-popular TV show: *Room 222.*

I got the job!

FOUR

High Hopes

Room 222 was one of the first shows featuring black actors in lead roles. The show was about teachers, students, and tolerance at Walt Whitman High School in Los Angeles. It was very popular and starred Lloyd Haynes, Denise Nicholas, Michael Constantine, and Karen Valentine.

I got this job on *Room 222* on November 22, having just turned twenty-two on August 22 of that year (cue eerie music). The brilliant James L. Brooks created the show and I read for him. He gave me the part of Rhoda Zagor right there in his office. I was so excited I jumped up on the coffee table. He didn't seem to mind. I would be called back to play this character two more times. In the first episode, my character, Rhoda, only had one line. When the teacher assigns a composition for the class to write, Rhoda raises her hand and asks, "You mean a 'you tell us what the topic is and we write a composition on it?'"

I remember this line vividly to this day, because I rehearsed it in front of the mirror for what seemed to be a thousand times, trying to make it funny. I said it *fast*. I said it *slow*. I put *emphasis* on different words. I made my voice go *up*. I made my voice go *down*. In the end I realized it was just a line with a lot of one-syllable words. It was as funny as it was going to get. Just say it!

I was looking forward to having my hair and makeup professionally done. It was something I had dreamed about. The production called me the day before I was scheduled to work and asked me to come in with my hair already done, which I did. Now it was just the professional makeup experience I was looking forward to. When I sat in the chair I waited for what seemed like hours to have my makeup applied and when the makeup artist was finished I looked in the mirror for the first time. I couldn't believe it. *I was orange!* I ran to the ladies' room and looked in the mirror. Yep! I was definitely orange! In fact, because of the shape of my face I very much resembled a small pumpkin. I stopped myself from crying. I pulled myself together and applied my own lipstick because I thought it would make a difference, but it didn't. I went back to the makeup man who was a tall, older gentleman that people on the set were referring to as "Shotgun." I told him I thought I looked orange.

He said, "Get in the chair, we'll powder you down!"

Powder me down? How on earth would that help? He gently started powdering my face. I heard crinkling and felt plastic. The powder puff was still in the wrapper.

"There we go!" he said.

"All done!"

I just didn't get it! I couldn't understand what was happening. And then I started hearing laughter. People were watching my reaction, and evidently this was some sort of an initiation for actors on their very first job. Once again, I'd been punked! This time by a guy named Shotgun! I tried to be a good sport about it and laughed along with everybody, but I was still concerned about my makeup. Was Shotgun just joking? Was he going to redo my makeup to help me appear more human and less fruitlike? Well *that* didn't happen! So much for the glamour of show business!

If memory serves me correctly, the next two times I played Rhoda on the show the story line involved me consoling my best friend during her breakup with her boyfriend. I had lines that were expository and helped move the story along. I was very proud that I had been asked back to play the character again. And I'm happy to tell you that on those next two shows my skin tone on camera was no longer orange. It was more along the lines of grammar school paste.

Carol had also been working on *Room 222* as an extra. We attended the cast party together. She introduced me to Ed Begley Jr. He was wearing a trick tie that he controlled from his pocket with a switch, making it flip around. I loved him immediately. The first thing he said to me was, "Hi, will you marry me?"

Honestly, I thought about it for a minute.

After the cast party that evening, Carol and I went with Ed to his house where he served us tea from an heirloom China tea set. And he also showed us his collection of Betty Boop cartoons. He once took me on a date in his Taylor-Dunn electric car, which in those days was one step above the horse and buggy! Even back then he was an environmentalist and a man with lightning-quick wit and charm.

One day I was driving in my neighborhood in Hollywood and saw that a crew of workers was in the middle of cutting down a beautiful old tree to (like Joni Mitchell lamented in her song) make way for a parking lot. The tree was 150 years old. I had driven past it many times and always slowed down to dote on its beauty. It was majestic. And now it was vulnerable. I slowed down and lowered my window. Just as I was about to shout out my protest I heard a voice shouting from the other lane. I looked over—it was Ed in his electric car giving them a piece of his mind. Other cars slowed and did the same. Traffic was backed up in both directions. Of course the bank was victorious and cut the beautiful tree down. Now you can draw money from a lovely ATM that sits where the tree used to live.

My career continued to chug along. I started getting small parts in television shows like *Barefoot in the Park, Nanny and the Professor*, and then in *Beware the Blob*, a low-budget movie directed by Larry Hagman in which my character is eaten by the blob in a drainpipe in Glendale. One of my favorite memories was being cast for a part in *Drive, He Said*, which was beautifully directed by Jack Nicholson. He cast Lynne as one of the cheerleaders and me as the girlfriend of the basketball team's manager. Lynne and I drove to Eugene, Oregon, to shoot the movie. Mine was a nonspeaking role. All I had to do was watch a basketball go through a hoop. As a director, Jack is every actor's dream; enthusiastic, encouraging, complimentary and with you every step of the way. As an actor, he embodies the true definition of "Movie Star"; fascinating, intelligent, and relatable.

The very first movie I ever worked on was for Roger Corman who was already a legend in the film business. He was the king of low-budget filmmaking, especially the horror genre. Name an actor in Hollywood and he or she most likely worked for him.

In 1970, Roger Corman cast me in a film that he was producing and directing. It was titled *Gas-s-s-s! Or It Became Necessary to Destroy the World in Order to Save It*. It was sandwiched in between two of the three other films he did that year, *Scream of the Demon Lover* and *Angels Die Hard*. I was very excited. It was going to be shot on location in Socorro, New Mexico, and Roger was directing it himself. How could I get so lucky?

Not only was this my first actual movie role, but it was the second time I'd ever been on a plane! The first time I was eight years old when my mother took my sister and me from Dallas to Los Angeles to visit her uncle Joe (my grandmother's brother). We only had one-way tickets. We took the bus back to Dallas. At eight years old I was thrilled to ride on an airplane. I couldn't sleep the night before we left. But instead of excitement, this time I was filled with dread because even though the idea of traveling to a location to shoot a movie was a thrilling one, I found that I had a fear of flying and the trip to the location in Socorro was a frightening experience. Carol drove me to the airport and asked me if I was going to be okay. I told her yes. She asked me to call home when I got there. I told her I would. She told me to make sure I did or they'd worry.

When I landed in Albuquerque it was very late in the afternoon. I was exhausted and I was suffering from white-knuckling. A crew member was waiting at the airport to drive me to where I would be staying in Socorro. Another actress, Tally Coppola (who was soon to be the famous Talia Shire) was also being picked up. We drove for what seemed like hours until we turned off the highway and onto an unpaved road and headed out into barren desert, dust flying all around the car. I could see a large neon sign up ahead. It was a wagon wheel with the words THE HUB blinking on and off in the center.

The driver pulled in and parked under the blinking sign. Tally and I didn't say much as we got out of the car and followed the driver. I noticed that *right* next door to the motel was Ramirez Mortuary. The driver led us both into one room. (Obviously, we were going to be roommates.) Inside, I had the sudden revelation that our room shared a common wall with the mortuary. I'm not certain which of us started crying first, but I know there were some tears involved. The driver told us that most everyone else on the production was staying in town at another motel. We were put here at The Hub because there weren't any rooms left at the other place—so much for the romance of filming a movie on location!

I remembered my sister's request and noticed there was no phone in the room. There wasn't much of anything in the room except eeriness! The driver brought our bags in and then left. Tally and I sat there on our individual sagging twin beds. We discussed the fact that only a wall separated us from a mortuary. We also discussed the fact that this room would make a perfect setting for one of Roger Corman's early horror genre movies. We made our peace with it and were about to unpack when the driver came back and told us that two of the crew members who were staying at the motel in town were going to switch with us. We were so grateful. On the drive into town I asked about a phone. I was told there were phones in the rooms, but that the switchboard at the motel shut down at 8:00 p.m. so I wouldn't be able to make a call until 6:00 a.m. the next morning. My sister was going to have to wait and wonder.

The new motel in Socorro was at the edge of town. When we arrived, the office and the café were locked up tight! It was pitch black. There were no lights on the highway the motel was situated on and hardly a car passing by. But the room was much better and since we had to work in the early morning, we went directly to bed and locked the door tightly.

In *Gas-s-s* I played Ben Vereen's soon-to-be "baby mama," Marissa. The story called for me to be about six months pregnant.

High Hopes

Unfortunately when I arrived on set in the morning, wardrobe was missing the undergarment that would make me appear pregnant. When the wardrobe girl informed me there was no "baby bump," I asked her what I was supposed to do. She said, "Let's look around for something."

I was due on the set in less than an hour. I thought of the pillows on the bed in my room. The wardrobe trailer was in the parking lot outside of our motel. I ran to my room, grabbed a pillow off the bed, and tried it. It was too big! I saw the throw pillow that sat on the little club chair in the corner, and tried it. It was the right size, but it was square. I took them both and ran back to wardrobe. First the wardrobe girl and I tried the bed pillow, but it kept taking on air until I looked eleven months pregnant. We tried the square throw pillow with my costume over it. I looked in the mirror and thought I might get away with it. I didn't have time to dawdle; they were calling me to the set. I stuffed the throw pillow into my underwear and went with it. During the three-week shoot my "baby bump" kept shifting around. It would either be too high or too low depending on what pair of underwear I was wearing.

It was wonderful fun working on *Gas-s-s-s*. The cast was great! Everyone was so talented and so much fun. And Roger Corman was easygoing, affable, and always had a smile on his face. Hollywood legend has it that Roger was very frugal And that once when he was producing a film, the production manager came to him and told him they were running over schedule and needed to buy more days. Roger took the script, calculated how much time each page took to shoot, randomly opened the script, and pulled out eight pages. The movie came in on time.

After the first day's shooting when I got back to the motel, again the switchboard was shut down for the night. I was unsettled with the notion of my sister and my mother worrying about me. I loved bunking with Tally. She was a wonderful person with a crazy, dry sense of humor. Tally could make me laugh and she had this knack of making the joke always on herself. She spoke highly of her brother, Francis. I realized he was the same director who had written and directed *You're a Big Boy Now*, one of my favorite movies ever!

The next morning the switchboard was down. I couldn't believe my luck. When we were driving to the location I saw a café on the same road about a mile from our motel. Outside was a phone booth. Ah-ha! I made a plan! I was going to collect change from everyone I possibly could and that evening if I still wasn't able to call from my room for whatever the reason, I would simply trot to that phone booth and call my sister. On the third night when I got back to the motel, I had just missed the switchboard operator. It didn't matter because this time I was loaded for bear! I had all kinds of change for my call. It was very cold when I took off down the road on foot to the café. As I trudged along the road, two police cars rushed past me with their lights flashing. It was now getting dark, and colder by the minute! The sun had almost set. I could see the cafe's neon BEER sign flashing up ahead. It reminded me of the good old days waiting in the cab of my father's truck in Irving! Finally I made it to the phone booth, happy to shut the door even though it didn't make it any warmer. The light came on. I took the receiver and put it up to my ear. As I did this, two more police cars rushed by with their lights flashing and sirens blaring. I pushed my hand into my pocket, grabbed some change, and placed it on the little shelf below the phone. I took a dime and dropped it into the coin slot. Nothing! No dial tone! Thinking the phone might need more than a dime, I fished a quarter out of the stockpile of change and dropped that into the coin slot. Nothing! I jiggled the cradle up and down and listened. Still dead silence! Well, well, well! I stood there thinking and shivering and noticed the sign blinking above the door that led into the bar. I wondered just what lurked on the other side. A payphone might be in there. If not, maybe they would let me use the business phone so I could place a collect call to my sister. I'll just mosey on in and, in the sweetest voice I can muster, ask to use the phone. I sized up the gravel parking lot I now had to cross to get to the door of the bar. Except for the neon sign casting a light onto the small gravel parking lot it was now officially dark. I weighed my options and was determined to make that call. I returned the receiver to the cradle. I gathered my change and my courage, left the faux security of the phone booth, and started walking across the parking lot.

That's when I realized I hadn't seen a single soul go in or come out of the bar. I also realized that the cars I saw parked here were up on cinder blocks and rusted out, clearly abandoned! Okay, maybe people haven't gotten here yet, but people may be working inside, setting up. I was about twenty or so feet from the door. The beer sign was bigger than I had originally thought. No one would run up an electric bill to keep a sign this large lit if the place was abandoned. I picked up my pace, but didn't allow myself to break into a run because running would indicate fear and I had to be brave so I could make the call home and let my family know I was safe. I got to the door.

Forcing myself, I took a deep breath, grabbed the door handle, and pulled. *It was locked!* The buzzing of the neon sign was all I could hear because it was the only noise to cut through the night. I froze. The thought struck me. *I shouldn't be here.* I did not want to see what was behind me. I had to will my legs to move. When I turned there was nothing except the same desolate gravel parking lot. It seemed even lonelier. Again I thought I shouldn't be here. I wanted to run but didn't. I walked methodically back to the road. The adrenaline rush in my blood was almost blinding me. I thought, if I see a car I'm going to flag them down and ask for a ride. When I finally got to the road I didn't feel any safer. There wasn't a car in sight. No headlights in either direction. I started walking back toward the motel. I had been walking for a minute or two when I saw headlights speeding in my direction. As the car got closer I raised my arms and started waving them down. They sped past. I picked up my pace. It was dark and cold except for the light of a million stars. Suddenly from behind me, I heard a car. I turned to again see lights coming toward me. The lights got closer and I could see that they were pulling up alongside me and stopping. It was a police car. I stopped. The officer rolled down his window.

"Miss, what are you doing out here?" he asked.

I told him my story and he said, "Get in. I'll give you a ride. You can't be out here! There's a manhunt on! We've just had a young girl about your age murdered up the road and we're looking for the killer." A chill ran up my spine. I jumped in the car and he dropped me off at the motel, watching me as I hastily ran into my room and bolted the door. I was shaking. The next morning I made sure I called home.

My mother answered and said, "Cindy, thank God! We were getting worried."

I didn't tell her about the night before. Just told her how much I was enjoying my experience making the movie.

We moved location and, with that, motels. One night I mentioned that the episode of *Room 222* that I was in was going to

High Hopes

be on. Bud Cort (who later would play Harold in Hal Asby's film *Harold and Maude*) insisted we all watch it. I wasn't especially happy about having a party for my one line, but Bud and Tally were insisting. And they were like a booster club! From our new motel room we watched "The Substitute Teacher" episode. They applauded when I came on and delivered my line. Personally I was horrified. First of all, my skin *was* orange and second, despite all my efforts, in no way was it humorous. All that going over and over that darn line and look where it got me. I sucked! But I didn't detect the slightest pause from Bud or Tally. They immediately commented on how good I was.

I finished my three weeks on *Gas-s-s-s* and was sad to leave my newly made friends. Taking the plane home I was much more relaxed about possibly falling from forty thousand feet to the ground. I had just worked in a Roger Corman film! I was in *show* business! I was a *working* actress! And then the plane hit *major* turbulence!

One lucky day my agent got me an audition with Bill Persky and Sam Denoff (creators of the TV show *That Girl!*) for a one-hour musical variety show called *The Funny Side*, hosted by Gene Kelly. I had loved him since I was a little girl and I saw him and Debbie Reynolds and Donald O'Connor in *Singin' in the Rain*. The thought of working with him was almost too good to be true. But it was going to be true, because I got the job. And I got the job because of the way I read one specific line. The setup was something like, "How did you know I was rich?" My line was, "Oh, I don't know, your alligator shoes?"

Bill and Sam told me that I was the only one who had put a question mark at the end of the line and made the joke work. The premise of the show was to take one subject each week and look at the funny side through five different couples using comedy sketches and musical numbers: a husband-and-wife couple played by John Amos and Teresa Graves; a blue-collar husband and wife played by Warren Berlinger and Pat Finley; the comedy team of Dick Clair and Jenna McMahon played the affluent husband and wife; and Bert Mustin and Queenie Smith played the elderly husband and wife.

It was like old home week for me because Michael Lembeck and I played the teenage husband and wife and we had been in the Theatre Arts department at LACC together. Michael Lembeck had a wonderful sense of humor and could sing and dance. I felt a great relief to be teamed with him because he was always solid, always encouraging, and never judgmental when I was off-key or out of step! And believe me there were many times when I was just that! The first day of rehearsal we met Gene Kelly, the host of the show. He asked us all to call him "Gene." I couldn't stop staring at him; all I could think of was *Singin' in the Rain*, *Brigadoon*, and *An American in Paris*.

We shot at NBC studios in the Valley. The soundstage was next to *The Tonight Show*'s. Sometimes I'd wander over there just to look at Johnny Carson's desk or into their prop department and sometimes I'd imagine myself on the show with Johnny. This was about to become a reality because our musical director had written a number for Michael and me to perform on *The Funny Side* called, "Naders Raiders," a tribute to Ralph Nader. Coincidentally Ralph Nader was scheduled to appear on *The Tonight Show*. Bill and Sam, along with NBC, came up with the idea to have Michael and I perform the song on *The Tonight Show* for Ralph Nader. I didn't want to do it. Really we hadn't rehearsed enough or done it on our own show yet. But everybody was so keen on it, what could I say? I just kept rehearsing with Michael. They called us over to *The Tonight Show* soundstage to rehearse. We realized we were shaky on the number. Now I think Michael was questioning it also, but we couldn't turn back. Then God, in his infinite wisdom, intervened. Our number was bumped because, with all the guests they had appearing, the show was running too long and there wouldn't be enough time to perform it. Thank you, Lord! We were both more than relieved.

Gene Kelly was very kind to me. One time he and I had a verse to sing together. During rehearsal he told me that we sang alike. We weren't great singers, but could carry a tune and sound pleasing. Gene choreographed a little dance move to go with the verse we sang together. When we shot the number it was amazing. We did sound great together. He wrapped his arms around me. We swayed and sang, and then I realized I was standing on his foot.

One week our guest star was Jack Benny. Michael and I had a little scene with him and Gene. I had forgotten to take the gum out of my mouth before rehearsal. And at one point I absentmindedly blew a bubble while Jack was going through his dialogue. He used it and did one of his fabulous double-takes. Everyone laughed. He asked me if I would do it again and blow a bubble for him when we shot the show. *Well, of course I would!* Oh my goodness, setting up one of Jack Benny's fabulous takes! What a privilege. I was so blessed to be on this show, but sadly, after only thirteen weeks, NBC canceled it. However it wasn't the last time I would work with the most wonderful Gene Kelly.

Shirley, I Jest!

In 1972 I was called in to meet with George Cukor to read for the part of Tooley in *Travels with My Aunt,* which would eventually star Maggie Smith and Alec McCowen. I'd read the book by Graham Green beforehand and had studied the lines to the best of my ability. I thought I was prepared, but I wasn't. He knew exactly what he wanted and expected you to deliver just that. He was blunt and told you exactly what he thought about you.

George Cukor is famously known for his talent in directing women. At the time his dear friend Katharine Hepburn was set to play the part of Aunt Augusta. I wasn't nervous at all when I went in. In fact I was unusually calm. I waited for my turn at bat in the outer reception area. The door to Mr. Cukor's office opened. An actress came flying out. She looked at me for a second and then fled out the door. Had I seen tears in her eyes? I put down the magazine I'd been thumbing through, reached into my purse, pulled out the script, and started to study it immediately.

"Cindy, you can go in," the secretary said.

I felt my heart rate rise!

George Cukor was standing. He never sat during the entire audition. He held the script. He would first peer at it and then at me, analyzing both of us. His scrutiny was made sharper by the bifocals that sat on the end of his nose. Each lens was like a *spyglass*! He wanted to hear me read almost immediately; no chitchat! I read the scene with someone he had provided. I didn't think I was very good when I was done. He gave me a gaze again, over his spyglasses. Okay! I'll admit it, I was afraid of him, but at the same time I was mesmerized. He was a strict and disciplined director who expected perfection from actors. I was still a rookie. I was so happy to leave and head home, away from Mr. Cukor's spyglass gaze! I had almost forgotten about the audition when a

High Hopes

week later, my agent called with news that I had the part. It was difficult for me to believe.

By this time Maggie Smith had replaced Katharine Hepburn as Aunt Augusta. I had been so over the moon at being in a movie that starred Katharine Hepburn and now in heaven being in a movie with Maggie Smith. I landed in Madrid jet-lagged and exhausted. In the last three days I had been cast as Tooley, gotten my very first passport, packed my suitcases, and was off to live in Madrid for two months. I'll never forget the address of the apartment the production company had arranged for me to stay in while I shot my part in *Travels*. *Trente y tres* Dr. Fleming Street. The apartment was in Madrid, a little on the outskirts. The street had a lively nightlife and a charming café next door.

I was on the sixth floor. Thumping disco music could faintly be heard from within the building somewhere. I was exhausted and went straight to my tiny bedroom. I only unpacked my nightgown and my toothbrush. I gave my teeth a good brushing, changed clothes and climbed into my bed. Before I could close my eyes and fall into a deep sleep, I became aware that someone was walking around in the room above me. They obviously were wearing high heels. Their floor, like mine, was wooden, not carpeted.

Click, click, click, click, click went the heels. Then again, *click, click, click.*

Then they stopped.

Silence.

Next I heard what sounded like a long string of pearls being dropped into a dish. I thought that this must be my upstairs neighbor coming home from perhaps the disco. *Click, click, click, click, click,* once again. I hoped she'd take those shoes off and get in bed. I needed to be up in the morning to meet Anthony Powell, the costume designer. He was taking me wardrobe shopping for the film.

Click, click and then silence for a moment.

Next, I swear I heard her unzip whatever frock she was wearing. I mean, I assumed it was a dress given the pearls. I heard her drop her shoes to the floor.

Finally! We can both go to sleep.

But wait! What's this?

Another set of feet, not heels this time, maybe loafers. They scuffled for a minute and then I could hear them also being dropped on the floor.

Ah! She's married!

Now all seemed quiet as I snuggled in. I'd brought my own pillow. Then, squeaking!

Oh no! Oh no! Please don't tell me they're getting romantic!

And, indeed they were, and for about ten minutes the squeaking prevailed. Then, silence.

They were off to sleep!

But no, wait. They were up.

Zip! Click, click, click, click, click.

Heels crossing the room and then loafers crossing the room. And pearls being taken out of the dish. Then two sets of feet left the bedroom.

Click, click, click, click, click, and the door closed.

It was midnight in Madrid! I had to get to sleep and I finally did.

Downstairs in the small lobby the next morning as I waited for the car to pick me up, I met Antonio the doorman. I immediately struck a bond with him. He was about forty, charming and friendly. I could only speak "pigeon" Spanish. But still, we communicated somehow with great ease. Then I met Clautilde, the switchboard operator who was from Barcelona, who spoke with a King Philippe lisp. I loved her immediately.

"Nice to meet you, Clautilde."

"Nithe to meet yoo, too, Theendy."

I stepped out of my building and into the car that had pulled up to take me to meet the wardrobe designer, Anthony Powell. Antonio held the door for me. At the same time a gypsy woman holding a baby followed by two young daughters came rushing up asking me for centavos. The baby reached out to me with one arm and the hand open as if begging. I started to reach into my purse when Antonio shooed them away. He looked at me and shook his finger back and forth as if to say *don't engage with them*. I felt sorry for them, and I knew if they sought me out again I would help them. It would just have to be away from the ever-watchful eye of Antonio.

I'm not, nor have I ever been, a fashionista by any stretch of the imagination. But shopping in Madrid for my character's wardrobe with Anthony Powell and being a size two was an incredible experience. (A little note here: Anthony would go on to win an Oscar for best costume design for *Travels with My Aunt*.) Anthony had a great wit as well as style. We shopped all afternoon!

I had the next day off. I decided to go to the Prado and peruse its vast and magnificent collection of Fine Art. That evening when I got home, as I got out of the cab I could see the gypsy woman and her children standing across the street being snubbed by passersby, and again I felt sad for them. I went upstairs and studied my script for a couple of hours. I was much too nervous to eat dinner so I climbed in bed and was just about to fall asleep when:

Click, click, click, click, click. She was back!

Click, click.

Silence.

Again, the sound of a string of pearls being dropped into a dish.

Then, *Zip! Click, click* and then she sat on the bed. And now for the other set of footsteps. This time I thought they sounded like boots. I waited. Ten minutes of squeaking ensued, then the dressing, *Zip! Clack, clack, clack,* the door closed, and they were gone.

I could *finally* go to sleep!

This went on every night the entire time I was in Madrid.

Two days later I was on the set waiting to shoot my first scene. I was sitting in my chair next to Mr. Cukor, outside the trailers. We were facing the sun. I had been told to always refer to him as "Mr. Cukor" or "Mr. Cukor, sir." He had summoned me earlier to go over my scenes. Trouble was, I couldn't see him due to the sun in my eyes and he wouldn't allow me to wear sunglasses. I could only make out the outline of his body. We went over the lines, what he wanted in the scene, the emotion, I made the suggestion of changing the word "fuzz" into "cops," telling him that "fuzz" was not really a term young people used anymore. I think he was glaring at me.

He sternly asked me: "What does it say in the script?"

"Fuzz," I answered.

"Then that's what you'll say."

We went on with the lesson.

I would read a line for him and he would say, "Again!"

I would read it again and he would say, "Again!"

After about a half hour of this, the man who had so brilliantly directed *The Philadelphia Story, Born Yesterday, Pat and Mike,* and let's not forget *Gaslight,* let me return to my trailer. I laid down in my trailer wondering why he had cast me in this part. Obviously I wasn't right for it except for my fabulous costumes!

I met Alec McCowen that day. We had the aforementioned "fuzz" scene to shoot together and I thoroughly enjoyed everything about him—his great sense of humor, his endless wit—and he was a marvelous actor. We were invited to have drinks at Mr. Cukor's suite at the Ritz-Carlton. I would have preferred not to go as I didn't want to come into his spyglass crosshairs again. I believe it was Alec who convinced me to go. I think we rode over together. The ornate suite was magnificent, with beautiful drapes and furniture. I don't know why, but I sat close to the door in case I needed to make a hasty exit! It was like the adults on one side and the kids on the other. I didn't want a drink-drink. When Mr. Cukor heard this he had them bring me tea, but not just *any* tea. He explained to me that it was tea that *Katharine Hepburn* had especially blended and sent to him. When the tea was served to me I just held onto the cup and stared into the tea. It was too precious to drink. Alec was in his element across the way, but I was thoroughly uncomfortable. Finally we left. I was happy to get home and into my bed. Happy to hear *click, click, click* again.

I would see Maggie Smith in the mornings going to makeup. She had hours of it while they tried to age her into the eighty-year-old Aunt Augusta. Something was making her unhappy. It seemed as though each morning when I would pass her on the stairs she was weeping. But she always managed a smile and a "Good morning, Cindy," for me. I found out later that the makeup artist she loved and trusted had been placed in another position, and the studio would bring in someone they thought was more experienced. That made this extraordinary actress very unhappy.

On my days off, I would walk along my street going into the café next door to drink the best coffee I've ever had. On one of these days the two little gypsy girls came up to me begging. I gave them some money and then asked them if they wanted to get an ice cream in the parlor up the street. Their eyes lit up and off we went. One of the girls was around six or seven and the other about ten. When I tried to enter the ice cream parlor with them, the owner shouted: "*¡Fuera! Fuera! No hay gitanos en aquí!*" ("Out! Out! No gypsies in here!")

Frightened, they ran outside. I ran after them. The little one was crying. I told them as best I could in my broken high school Spanish not to worry and asked them both what kind of ice cream they wanted. I said I'd get it for them. Each wanted strawberry. With them waiting outside, I marched back in and ordered the biggest strawberry ice-cream cones I could buy. I glanced at them through the window, waiting. They were dirty and in rags. The same man that shouted at them told me to stay away from them.

Once outside, I gave them their cones and told them to follow me. At the other end of my street was a Woolworths. My plan was to take them in and buy them each a new dress or whatever I could find when they were finished with their cones. As we walked I could see their mother with her begging baby on the other side of the street. I wondered if she worried about her two young daughters being out here. But then it was probably she who sent them to me with no thought of keeping them close to her. We got to Woolworths. We stood in the doorway. I didn't want to enter before we had permission. I didn't want a repeat of the ice cream parlor incident. I asked a clerk if they had children's clothing. Somehow I managed to get across to the clerks that I wanted to bring in the children and buy clothes for them.

High Hopes

The clerk said, "*Si*."

I guess the idea of a sale overrode whatever gypsy prejudice she had. We were welcomed in. The children and I made our way to the clothing racks and they were ecstatic about selecting new clothes. I gathered clothing that I thought would be appropriate for them and with our arms loaded down with the new duds we went into the dressing rooms. First, I helped the little one try on the sweetest sundress. She was thrilled! It was perfect. Next I started helping the older child out of her tattered dress. She had chosen a dress and a pair of pants. She signaled to me that she could do it herself. I stayed in the room with them. She gave me an embarrassed look as she took her skirt off. It was then that I realized that this sweet little girl was a little boy! I made no notice of it and bought him the pants and the dress; or should I say the costume that I realized his mother dressed him in to garner more pity and more money. All that mattered in the end was that they had a bit of happiness. From that day on I was known on my street as "*La Loca Americana*."

The night before my big scene with Alec McCowen on the Orient Express the *click, click, clicking* continued. My girlfriend upstairs was *muy, muy* busy! Finally when she took her rest, I couldn't. Between her and the anticipation of the scene in the morning, I barely had a wink of sleep. The next day I tried to avoid Mr. Cukor. I was afraid he was going to give me another "lesson in the sun." He was sitting in his director's chair in the common area outside the dressing room trailers where he always sat with a script rolled up in his hand and an empty chair positioned directly across from him. I slithered along a building flattening myself as much as possible, trying to disappear.

The production assistant came walking straight to me and yelled, "Found her!"

Shirley, I Jest!

I was escorted to my seat in the "sun." For an hour we went over and over the script with Mr. Cukor telling me how Tooley might be feeling. There were degrees of emotion in the scene that he intended to wrench out of me.

Finally he asked me, "Do you know your lines?"

"Yes!"

"Do you know your lines?"

"Yes, sir!"

"Good! Now forget them!"

Mr. Cukor dismissed me. I walked to my trailer and climbed onto my bed. I was so anxious I fell asleep with my eyes open. They came to get me to shoot the scene. "Difficult" does not even begin to describe the experience. The more Mr. Cukor drove my emotions, the less I could give. During takes I could see him acting the scene out. I would cry between takes. The makeup artist would wipe the tears away and we'd go again. Once, Douglas Slocombe, the cinematographer, said he couldn't shoot because I had tears rolling down my face. Alec was so kind to me, whispering that he thought it was fine. Take after take we'd work until the words became a jumble of consonants and vowels. Finally he called it a day and I was released to go home. I was shaking and that night I was comforted to hear my friend from upstairs *click, click, clicking.*

When I got back to the States a few weeks later, I learned that the street I'd been living on was called Dr. Fleming because it was in the notorious Red Light District of Madrid and Dr. Fleming was the physician who treated the prostitutes for venereal disease. The street was named for him.

Click! Click! Click!

FIVE

Some Enchanted Evening

American Graffiti was George Lucas's first studio film. Written by Gloria Katz, Willard Huyck, and George Lucas, the story mirrored, in many ways, his high school experiences. The movie was set as a "coming of age" story at a beautiful time of our country's innocence; before the Vietnam War, before the assassination of President Kennedy, and before technology ruled our daily lives. The film was shot in twenty-eight nights and one morning. The budget was $775,000, most of that used to acquire the rights to the iconic music that would run throughout the film. The movie had a young cast of basically unknowns and a young director, no makeup budget, and no dressing rooms. However, one Winnebago was parked in whatever empty spot or vacant lot Gary Kurtz, the film's coproducer, could find at the time. The Winnebago housed the costumes and the hairdresser, who only styled the wigs. A station wagon was the only means of transportation to and from the set. It also carried props and was driven by a kid who was (for some reason) very territorial and protective of the rides he parsed out to the cast. If you were finished for the night and the station wagon wasn't available, you could wait an hour, or it could be until dawn before you'd get that ride back to the Holiday Inn. On these occasions I would sit and wait on the couch in the Winnebago, under the costumes that hung on the rack overhead.

Because the movie took place in one night, we shot from sundown to sunup, 6:00 p.m. to 6:00 a.m. And I know no one will believe this, but you know that old Hollywood saying, "pull the plug"? A guy, who was sent by Universal, would sit by the generator and at precisely 6:00 in the morning, on the dot, he would pull the generator plug, halting production to make sure the film would come in on time and on budget, no matter what.

My personal adventure with *American Graffiti* began when I returned from Spain after *Travels with My Aunt*. I was still reeling from the experience as well as suffering from extreme jet lag. I had no sooner landed in L.A. and crawled into bed when the phone rang. Calling was my friend, Fred Roos. He was casting a movie and wanted to send over a script; and needed me to read it as soon as possible. The script was titled *American Graffiti*.

"*American* what?" I asked.

"Graffiti," Fred said. I asked him what that meant.

"Just read it as soon as it gets there! It's great! The director is a young guy out of USC. He's excellent. You're gonna want to be in this movie. Look over the role of Laurie."

I tried to protest, citing my jet lag, but he wouldn't let me. So when the script arrived, bleary-eyed, I read it. And I loved it. There was only one problem, I told Fred when I called him. I didn't want to play the part of Laurie Henderson, the ingénue. I wanted to play Debbie, the fast girl. He told me that Candy Clark had already been cast in that part.

I said, "Okay, then how about Carol?"

"Carol is supposed to be twelve," Fred said.

"I'll put braces on my teeth."

He told me that as silly as it seemed, he had to cast an actual twelve-year-old to play that part! (The part went to Mackenzie Phillips.) I told him of course, I was joking, but I really didn't want to play Laurie because all she does is sulk and cry throughout the entire movie.

"It's a great part," Fred insisted. "I need you at Universal tomorrow at 11:00 a.m. to meet the director."

I gave in and said, "All right, send me the address." The next morning I find myself sitting across from this kid in his office at Universal Studios, while he peruses my 8×10 photo. Maybe a minute of silence passes, I might have even fallen asleep before he looks up at me and says one word: "Terrific!"

And just like that, George Lucas had asked me to come back the next day to screen test for the role of Laurie. When I got home, I called Fred once again, and told him there is no way I could memorize the test scene by tomorrow.

He told me, "You can hold the script." I insisted I couldn't do it because of the jet lag and my nerves and not knowing the lines.

He says, "You have to, I'm down to the wire trying to cast this part. I've already teamed you up with Ron Howard."

"Ron Howard. OPIE?"

"Yes," Fred says.

Now, I love Ron Howard, honestly, I loved him in *Mayberry RFD*, *The Andy Griffith Show*, and *The Music Man*, and he was brilliant in *The Courtship of Eddie's Father* with Glenn Ford. But I still resisted, and then Fred throws the curve ball.

"Oh, did I tell you Francis Coppola is producing?"

"Well, this is the first time I've heard about Francis Coppola producing."

Shirley, I Jest!

Although I had not seen *The Godfather* yet, I was a huge fan of the movie *You're a Big Boy Now*. I had seen it four times when I was at City College, working at the IHOP across the street from the movie theater. I have to admit, I was impressed!

The next day I was holding my script, slow dancing with Ron Howard at Haskell Wexler's studio in Hollywood. I was dragging and nervous and thought *I'll probably blow this and they won't hire me anyway and I can just sleep the rest of the week!* Earlier when I had arrived, I was introduced to Ron Howard who would be playing Steve Bolander, Laurie Henderson's high school sweetheart. I liked him right off the bat. He was genuinely a nice guy! We went over the lines together, and then I told him that I was sorry, but I had to hold my script. He told me not to worry, that it was fine with him. George and Ron and I discussed the scene a little before the take. George was so calm, or was it that he was an innately quiet person? Whatever it was, he seemed confident and it rubbed off on me and helped me get through the scene. When it was over we were out the door. Ron and I said our good-byes and I got in my car and shook. Even though I was reluctant about this part, the actress in me wanted it, and I felt as though I had blown it. But I hadn't! I was offered the part almost immediately when I got home and walked through the door. I was thrilled! The actress in me trumped doubt and jet lag!

George asked for a meeting with Ron and me. He wanted to talk over our story line and explain his vision for the movie. Sitting across from him in his office at Universal, I remember thinking, *he's young and old all at the same time.* He explained that they didn't have a budget for makeup, hair, or dressing rooms. This didn't seem to concern Ron or George. I, on the other hand, was slightly worried about the six-year age difference between Ron

Some Enchanted Evening

and me. I might need just a little help to look seventeen! (I was twenty-four at the time and Ron just turned eighteen.) George had our 8×10's on his desk, side by side. I kept glancing at them, trying to see if we looked real as a teen couple. Right before we got up to leave, George made a point of telling us that he saw this movie as a "musical" because the songs would not stop except for a couple of dramatic points. Once, when the car is stolen and the source of the music is the car radio, which is gone; and the second time at the end when the race abruptly ends because the '55 Chevy flips over.

As Ron and I left and walked down the hall at Universal we looked at each other and almost in sync said, *"A musical? That's genius!"*

In June 1972 I found myself driving my orange Karmann Ghia into San Francisco, a city I knew from my days as a hippie. The sky was foggy and I loved it. I headed across the Golden Gate Bridge into Marin County toward the San Rafael Holiday Inn where the cast would be staying. The Marin County Courthouse was on my right. (At that very courthouse Angela Davis was now on trial for aggravated kidnapping and first-degree murder. She was later acquitted.)

We hit the ground running. We shot the opening scene of the film at Mel's Drive-In, on Lombard Street in San Francisco (unfortunately the diner has since been torn down). The very first shot was of Charlie Martin Smith driving on his Vespa. Charlie played Toad, everybody's affable friend, who was in for a long night with the fast girl, "Debbie," played by Candy Clark. George wanted to get this shot as the sun went down. Charlie didn't know how to drive the Vespa, and had to be given one quick lesson by Harry Travers, the transportation manager. Then they had to roll. If you've ever seen the movie, you'll see Charlie crashing the Vespa into the trash can in front of Mel's Drive-In. George kept rolling. Charlie deftly reacts, leaves the Vespa, and without missing a beat, walks away. George had no time for a second take with the sun quickly setting. So of course, this take stayed in and opens the movie.

The City of San Rafael hosted our next location. While the cameras rolled, classic cars circled the little town all night long. The constant revving of engines and peeling out of tires echoed for two nights straight while actors shouted their lines at each other through open car windows. Something about the commotion made the city leaders jumpy. After that second night, the film company was asked to leave. The production moved to Petaluma, a city that welcomed us with open arms and we arrived like a band of gypsies—Winnebago, station wagon, hot rods, and all!

One week into filming we were shooting a scene in the '58 Impala. Ron and I were being towed by the camera truck. When the scene ended we waited to hear George yell "*Cut!*" but nothing came. We waited a few seconds longer and then the camera operator shook George's shoulder to wake him up. He was so tired from shooting all night and editing all day he had actually fallen asleep sitting on the tow car. Many times after George yelled "Cut," Ron and I would ask, "How was it, George?"

Without fail, George always gave the same one-word response. "Terrific!"

The film had a soul of its own. All of these beautiful machines represented classic American craftsmanship that was bedazzling— the '32 Deuce Coupe, the '55 Chevy, an art form of motion. Sometimes before takes, Haskell Wexler, the great cinematographer and director (who was working as George's visual consultant), would take a cloth and polish certain parts of the cars. I asked him one time why he did this? He told me this would bounce light off the cars during the shots and make them sparkle. And it did! It made them shimmer brilliantly. If you've seen the film, you know what I'm talking about. The look was American eye-candy.

One night while we were waiting to shoot a scene, Ron and I sat in the '58 Chevy Impala. Ron got out of the car and went to where the camera crew was setting up. I watched him speak intently with Haskell for a while. When he got back in the car I asked him what they were discussing. Ron told me he was asking Haskell about the setups and the shots because one day *he* wanted to direct!

"Oh, great!" I said. But I was really thinking, *"What's he talking about, directing? He's so young to be thinking about directing!"* I am embarrassed to be sharing this thought since we all know he went on to accomplish great work *behind* the camera.

On one particularly cold night while I was waiting to shoot a scene, a seat wasn't to be found in the Winnebago. I noticed the station wagon parked nearby. I walked over and tried the handle. It was open. I didn't want to get in trouble (because the kid was so strict about the use of that car), but the cold and dark overrode any trouble the kid might cause me. I just needed a place to sit. I scooted into the driver's seat. I was enjoying the solitude when suddenly a figure popped up from the backseat. It scared me and I jumped! It was Harrison Ford! He'd been sleeping. We looked at each other and started laughing.

"What are you doing here?" he asked.

"Waiting to work," I replied. "There was no room in the Winnebago."

"Yeah, I know," he said. "I'm finished for the night, but the kid won't give me a ride home, so I'm waiting in here."

Harrison laid back down and I waited in silence. The funny picture of how I met Harrison a year before popped into my head. A mutual friend had introduced us in a health food store in Hollywood. Harrison was barefoot and buying organic vegetables.

A few nights later, Harrison and I had a little scene to shoot together where Laurie decides to get in the car with his character, Falfa, the bad boy who has come into town to challenge John Milner, played by Paul Le Mat. While we were sitting in the '55 Chevy waiting to begin, Harrison started singing "Some Enchanted Evening" just like Rossano Brazzi. It made me laugh! I suggested he sing it to me at the end of the scene. He did and George liked it, and tried to use it in the movie. In fact, there was talk about changing the title of the movie to *Some Enchanted Evening*, but George was not granted the rights by the license holders. Ultimately, they did allow the song to be included and it was edited back into the film.

One evening the kid picked me up to drive me to the set. He told me that we needed to make a detour first, to pick up one other person who was working that night. We headed to Sausalito and picked up a young woman named Suzanne Somers who was going to play the part of the blonde in the white T-Bird who says "I love you" to Curt (Richard Dreyfuss). When she climbed into the station wagon with us I was stunned. She was one of the prettiest people I'd ever seen! I could tell that the kid was smitten.

As pretty as she was, she was just as nice. We introduced ourselves, and I asked her if she was an actress. I thought they'd hired a model to play the part. She answered, "Yes," and many years later she told me she was taken aback by my question and had thought about it that whole night. Looking back on it now, without my having told her that I thought she was a model, I could see how it could have come off sounding insensitive. When we got to the set, I ushered her into my "dressing room" (the couch under the wardrobe rack) where we talked for a while.

Years later she told me this little story about filming that night. She had gone over and over her one line, "I love you," trying it many different ways in the mirror at home. When she was sitting in the T-Bird about to film, George came over to her and said, "I just want you to mouth the line." After all that rehearsing, she wasn't going to actually speak the line, not knowing then that it would become one of the most iconic moments in the film.

Richard Dreyfuss played my brother, Curt. I met Richard when I was nineteen. He and my friend, Lynne Stewart, had gone from grade school through high school together, and they had been neighbors. Lynne introduced us one afternoon when we were at her parents' house. Lynne called him Ricky and that's how she introduced him to me. And to this day when I see him, I have to make an effort to refer to him as Richard. As fate would have it, Lynne was cast in *American Graffiti* as Bobbie Tucker and she and Richard have a wonderful scene together.

I had a day off and was spending it in my hotel room going over my lines when someone knocked on my door. I opened it to find Richard standing there sporting a black eye!

"Cindy, do you have any makeup?" he asked.

"I have some concealer," I said.

"Can I use it? I'm shooting tonight and I need to cover *this* up."

I had him step in and I applied the cover-up. It worked pretty well. I asked him what happened. He explained it this way, "It involved some beer, rowdy behavior, and the shallow end of the hotel pool."

Shirley, I Jest!

Halfway through production George assembled twenty minutes of the film, put to music, and invited the cast to see it. Up until this point everyone pretty much thought they were doing a low-budget car movie. But holy smokes, after seeing what George had put together with the score we were all rendered speechless. Except for someone who shouted out, "This is unbelievably *great!*" And it was! If anyone had expectations, this exceeded them. It was a thing of beauty.

George was under tremendous pressure to finish the film. Ron, Paul Le Mat, Charlie Martin Smith, Harrison Ford, and I were on Paradise Road shooting the start of the drag race scene between Falfa and his black '55 Chevy and Milner in his yellow Deuce Coupe. The script called for Laurie to ride along with Falfa, defying Milner's protest. Toad starts the race with the signal of the flag. Onlookers watch as the cars fight each other with attitude and speed, barreling toward the finish line. Suddenly the '55 loses control and careens off the shoulder of the road, rolling into a field and catching fire, Laurie and Falfa's fate unknown. George shot the first part of the scene cutting just before the '55 careens. Ron and I were dismissed and walked back to the Winnebago. We had no sooner started to change out of our costumes when the first assistant director came running up to the Winnebago door shouting for us to stop.

"George wants to shoot the end of the scene right now! He has to get it before the sun gets too high." We protested, arguing with him while we put our costumes back on. "You'll have to talk to George about it, all I know is we need you to hurry!"

Ron and I were in a panic. We'd been caught off-guard. This part of the scene was not scheduled to be shot today. We made a mad dash for the field where George was standing with Haskell

Some Enchanted Evening

and the crew. Harrison and Paul were gathered around. The sun was coming up!

Ron and I spoke over each other at the same time, "George, we weren't scheduled to shoot this scene today. We're not ready, we haven't rehearsed!"

George said, "I have to shoot it now while I have the cars in position. If it doesn't work, we'll come back and re-shoot it."

At this point we all knew that was a fairy tale. There were simply no more sunrises available on the schedule to shoot the end of this complex scene. And then there was *that guy* sitting by the generator looking at his watch. George continued (and I paraphrase): *Look, we have to make it work, because at the end of the credits there won't be a line that reads: "This movie was shot in twenty-eight nights for no money under extremely difficult conditions."*

In other words, we had no excuses. It was do-or-die. The sun was rising and we needed to improvise, and improvise well. They had the '55 in place and flipped over with a crew member standing by ready to make it look like it was on fire. George explained the shot was basically going to be an all-in-one. I'd be up the hill with Harrison. Ron and Paul would run up the hill toward the car. Ron would get me and walk me down the hill to safety. Haskell would follow us with the steady-cam as we played our dialogue out.

Harrison and I ran to our beginning marks; the car was already on fire.

I said, "I'm going to take swings at you with my purse, is that okay, Harrison?"

And just as Harrison says, "Sounds good!" we heard George yell, "Action!"

I grabbed Harrison's shirt and started striking at him with my purse. Harrison held me at arm's length. Ron and Paul ran up and separated us. Ron grabbed me and we started down the hill as Haskell and the sound people followed us. It turned out to be one of my favorite scenes.

After the movie wrapped, Francis Coppola and his wife, Ellie, invited the cast for an evening cruise on the San Francisco Bay. Everyone went, even George! It was a beautiful evening on the water. I believe there was a full moon. When we docked at the Embarcadero, George did not have the seventy-five cents to pay for the ferry ride back to Marin County. I loaned it to him. Well, we all know the upshot to *this* Cinderella story. Not too many years would pass before George would end up with enough money to buy the ferry boat *and* Marin County if he wanted to!

When all was said and done, Universal held onto the film and did not give it a proper release until word of mouth by Universal employees who had seen a screening started to sing its praises. After the film's eventual release it was an overnight hit with lines around the block and sold-out performances at movie theaters. It was dubbed the first "Summer Blockbuster."

I called Richard Dreyfuss who was on location in Canada shooting *The Apprenticeship of Duddy Kravitz*. I told him about the phenomena going on. He didn't believe me. I assured him it was true. He would understand soon enough because aside from its enormous critical acclaim and financial super success, the honors would include his own Golden Globe nomination for Best Motion Picture Actor—Musical/Comedy. George was nominated for Best Director—Motion Picture, Paul Le Mat won for Most Promising Newcomer—Male, and the film won Best Motion Picture—Musical/Comedy.

Although nominated, *American Graffiti* did not win the Academy Award for Best Picture. However, there were several more

Some Enchanted Evening

nods. George along with Willard Huyck and Gloria Katz were nominated for Best Writing, Story and Screenplay, Candy Clark was nominated for Best Actress in a Supporting Role, and Verna Fields and Marcia Lucas were nominated for Best Film Editing.

I had underestimated the power of the Laurie Henderson role because, lo and behold, I was nominated for Best Supporting Actress by the British Academy of Film and Television Arts (BAFTA), their sole nomination for the film. An honor I still can't believe to this day!

But of all the accolades this little low-budget film garnered, to me the most formidable and dazzling would be this:

In 1995 *American Graffiti* was deemed culturally, historically, and aesthetically significant by The United States Library of Congress and selected for preservation in the National Film Registry.

Ain't that neat?

From right to left: My mother, my father, Cousin Marian. I don't know the other two, but aren't my momma and daddy a handsome couple?

My dad with me as a baby in California before my mother moved us to Texas.

First grade school picture taken in the dress my grandmother made out of a chicken feed sack.

My grandmother, me, my brother Jimmy and his wife Loretta, Mama, Carol, and Daddy.

My sister, Carol, my mother, Francesca, and me in Texas.

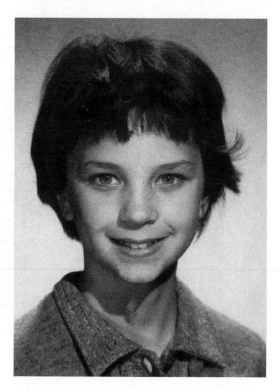

Me as Alfred E. Newman. I was 13 and while trying to cut my bangs, I sneezed.

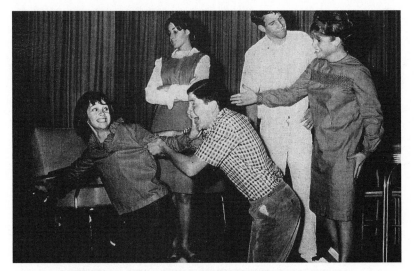

Our production of *Anne Frank* in high school.

Me dressed in my trusty beige wrap around skirt and ill-fitting white blouse. I'm certain that I'm wearing those black patent leather pumps too.

Lynne Stewart, Ed Begley, and me after riding the tram in Palm Springs.

Ron and I standing outside of Dewey High School in *American Graffiti*. Courtesy of Universal Studios Licensing, LLC

Me (Laurie) and Ron (Steve) slow dancing at the sock hop in *American Graffiti*. Courtesy of Universal Studios Licensing, LLC

The first season cast of *Laverne & Shirley* includes Carol Ita White, Phil Foster, Eddie Mecca, Betty Garrett, David Lander, Michael McKean, Penny, and me. Courtesy of CBS Television Studios

We could make suggestions to the writers of things we'd like to do and they would try to work it into the show. Penny suggested we somehow get hung on hooks. This is a picture of us trying to get off said hooks. Courtesy of CBS Television Studios

We bought into Lenny and Squiggy's dead uncle Lazlo's diner and now we're trying to make a go of it. Courtesy of CBS Television Studios

Laverne and Shirley go to a fat farm, get swaddled, and try to stand up by any means possible, ergo Penny pulling me up by the hair. Courtesy of CBS Television Studios

This is me, Ron, Henry, and Penny from a crossover show, meaning they appeared on our show. It was called "Shotgun Wedding." I like it because it's the four of us. Courtesy of CBS Television Studios

This is a picture of my mother and me on stage in a *Laverne & Shirley* Shotz talent show. My mother sang "Pennies from Heaven." Note the baskets on her hips they were filled with pennies, which she threw up in the air when she sang (see the pennies on the floor). She didn't get hurt. Courtesy of CBS Television Studios

I love this picture. It's taken from the "Fabian" show. We've snuck into Fabian's hotel suite under the guise of being hotel maids. When we hear security coming, we try to hide in a drawer. Courtesy of CBS Television Studios

The "Fabian" show. After not being able to attend his concert. Fabian sings "Turn Me Loose" to us privately in his hotel suite. I am pounding my head on the floor in ecstasy. (I stole the actions from my friend Ed Begley's stand-up routine about a stoned-out rocker.) Courtesy of CBS Television Studios

Troy Donahue was my dream guy when I was in my early teens. When I saw him in *Gidget* all I could think about was making out with him. This is a picture of a dream coming true. Courtesy of CBS Television Studios

In our living room in Milwaukee. Penny making me hit myself with my own hand. Courtesy of CBS Television Studios

Just stare at our faces. Courtesy of CBS Television Studios

Taken at the Sherry-Netherland in New York. John Belushi pretended to be using Penny's huge speakers as headphones while listening to E.L.O.

My friend Edna.

Ed Begley and me in the 1980s.

SIX

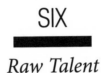

Raw Talent

The Conversation was referred to with love and humor by a small circle of friends as the movie Francis Coppola was making in between *Godfathers*. It was shot in eight weeks in San Francisco, and I was lucky enough to be cast (opposite Frederic Forrest) as Ann, the female half of the couple Gene Hackman's character Harry Caul is spying on and believes is going to be murdered.

On one of the first days of shooting I wasn't scheduled to work, but I was invited to drop by the set and say hello. The set was located on one of the highest floors of the Trans America building, which had not yet been completed. And on this day it was also predicted that California would experience a catastrophic earthquake and fall into the sea. I have to admit I was nervous about this prediction. And it was made eerier with the clear, plastic tarps hanging everywhere. I stood there mulling over the possibility that I could be floating out to sea like a Viking before the day was done. When who appeared all gussied up in his preppy clothes and haircut but Harrison.

Shirley, I Jest!

He greeted me by whispering, "I'm trying to get them to buy me a $300 suit to wear in this movie, but wardrobe says they don't have the budget."

"A $300 suit?" I asked.

"Yeah, I think my character would wear an expensive suit."

Before I could respond he was gone; called to the set for rehearsal. The set was very exciting and no one seemed to be worried about the prediction but me. As the day went by I realized I was not going to become part of the Lost Continent.

My first day of shooting was in Union Square. I remember watching Francis directing background actors for the opening scene. He went to each person or couple individually and very quietly gave them each a direction; a backstory, subject, or personal theme he wanted them to be discussing during the scene. If you see the movie, you will notice how seamlessly natural and interesting the people are as they move around Union Square in the background. And you might catch snippets of their conversations. I believe this was part of Francis's vision for the movie. He had said sometimes you might overhear a part of a conversation and assume things to be true that aren't. This is the very thing that undoes Harry Caul, Gene Hackman's character.

While we were shooting I came down with the flu (the Russian flu, to be exact). I felt awful about having to stay in bed, at the hotel. I knew the production schedule would have to be rearranged, and they were already having trouble with the city because of the fog machines they were running in the park. But I was too sick to stay on my feet. At the time, I wasn't sure who did this, but two days into my illness there was a knock at my door. I stumbled around to answer it. I asked who it was.

A man from the other side of the door said, "I'm a violinist and I've been sent here to play for you."

Raw Talent

I opened the door a little and he handed me a card. I was too bleary-eyed to read it. But from what I could make out, he had been hired to play for me. I told him I had the flu. The Russian flu!

He said, "Miss, I've been paid a lot of money to play for you."

"All right," I said. "Come in, but try and keep your distance. I would feel terrible if you caught this from me."

I climbed back into bed.

He stood as far away as he could from the foot of my bed and for half an hour this lovely musician played the most beautiful music. I wanted to tip him, but he wouldn't allow it. I don't think he wanted to touch my hand! Then, he was gone. When I was feeling better, I read the card and it was Frederic and Harrison who had sent him. I was so flattered, I blushed.

We were back in the park shooting with the fog machines (by now the production had been granted permission by the city to operate them). The scene involved Harry Caul following me through the park in the fog until I got halfway up a flight of cement steps. Francis directed me to stop at one point, turn around and give Harry a look as if to say: *If you continue following me, I will run up these steps and disappear in this fog.* I tried it twice and wasn't getting it.

Francis said, "Cindy, try this. Run all the way up the steps except for the last two. When you stop, turn and look at him, then start to take the next step." On the next take I followed his direction, and he was right. That did the trick.

The movie and Francis were nominated for numerous awards: Best Picture, Best Writing, Original Screenplay, Best Sound. At the Cannes Film Festival, Francis won the prestigious Palme d'Or. Not bad for a little movie that was in between *The Godfathers.*

After the two-year roll I had been on with *Travels with My Aunt*, *American Graffiti*, and *The Conversation*, my career seemed to slow down. In 1974 Tom Gries hired me to play Betty, a cannery worker in a wonderful movie of the week titled *The Migrants*. The movie starred Cloris Leachman, Ron Howard, Sissy Spacek, and Ed Lauter. The story was about a family of migrant workers struggling to exist through poverty and emotional strife, and believe it or not once again I played Ron's girlfriend. We shot the movie in Vineland, New Jersey, and one afternoon when we had a day off, Ron was antsy and borrowed a production vehicle to go for a drive. Sissy and I came along. Sissy fell asleep in the backseat while Ron drove and I tried my hand at navigating using my Native American skills, so it's not surprising when we ended up lost in Atlantic City an hour later! We stopped to regroup, parking outside a place called the Le Boo Lodge, but not a lodge in a hotel sense, more like a moose or elk lodge. Ron was intrigued.

"The Le Boo Lodge," he said. "What do you think that's all about?"

"I don't know," I said, looking at the sign. We looked in the backseat and Sissy was still asleep. I had a slightly ominous feeling. I think Ron did too. We decided to find our way back to Vineland. We retraced the route we had taken, but we were out in the countryside and the sun was now going down. We realized we needed help. We pulled into the parking lot of a roadside bar. Two men spilled out of the door and onto the gravel parking lot arguing. Ron and I were startled, but made the decision to respectfully ask them for directions.

As soon as they were finished with their argument, Ron politely called one of the men over and said, "Excuse me, could you tell us how to get to Vineland?"

Raw Talent

The guy hesitated, and looked us over. He was obviously drunk. Did he recognize Ron? He was friendly enough in a scary kind of way when he said, "OK! You'ze makes a jug handle outta here, go down about two miles. Cross the railroad tracks. Now you're travelin' west. You'll see 40 up ahead. Just follow that until you see signs for Vineland. OK?"

"Right! Got it! Thank you! Thank you!" Ron said. We left the parking lot and Ron turned to me and asked, "What's a jug handle?"

"Well," I said, "I guess," (I put my hand up and curved it.) "It's like a handle on a jug!"

And so we made a semicircle out of there. And the directions proved to be perfect. We made it back to Vineland, with Sissy still sleeping in the back, blissfully unaware of her southern New Jersey misadventure. *The Migrants* turned out to be a critical success. It was, however, one of the last jobs I would have for a long, long time.

I was running out of money and headed toward "broke." The success of *American Graffiti* had been phenomenal. George Lucas had been very generous and had taken one of his gross points from the movie and divided it equally, giving one-tenth of a point to each of the top ten cast members. This income supported me for a year.

Then I got a part on a TV show called *Insight*. I played a teenager who found herself pregnant and was in crisis about having her baby. That baby was played by none-other-than Mr. Ron Howard. Yep! Ron was my son waiting in heaven to be born, while I struggled with a health and moral dilemma on earth. We didn't have a scene together. He would have looked pretty ridiculous swaddled in a blanket lying in my arms.

Shirley, I Jest!

Traditionally the show's producer, Father Kaiser, handed you your paycheck personally and if you so choose to, you handed it back to him for Catholic Charities. At this time I could have really used the money. As the wonderful smiling priest handed it to me, I had the mortal thought of grabbing it and running before either of us could say "Hail Mary!" But I didn't. My Methodist Catholic guilt got the best of me and I dutifully handed it back. He graciously thanked me. Boy, I could have used that money at the time. As I was leaving Father Kaiser's office, Ron was coming in. We greeted each other, and I wondered if he knew the drill. I also wondered if Ron would give up *his* paycheck. I never found out.

During this period, I auditioned for:

The Rocky Horror Picture Show: I was up for the part of Janet. I was certain I could land it. I loved this script. It was so different, filled with high-camp characters and great music. I was told after the initial audition they wanted to see me again, and prepare to sing "Over at the Frankenstein Place." Then I would be reading a scene with Tim Curry. My agent called and told me it was between Susan Sarandon and me. I was so happy even though there was that little *Susan Sarandon thing* to get around. My audition was scheduled for 1:00 p.m. at the Roxy nightclub on the Sunset Strip (my old stomping grounds). I got there a little early and was asked to sit in one of the booths near the stage. I was looking over my script when I hear a female voice singing "Over at the Frankenstein Place." I look over and see Susan Sarandon on the stage singing away. I try to slump down in my seat. I don't want her to see me halfway through the number. It might throw her. It would be unfair. But then again, I didn't want to be there at all because she was good and it was throwing my confidence off. Someone had made a scheduling blunder. When her audition was over I put my fingers in my ears so I wouldn't be able to hear any comments from the director, Jim Sharman. But I did and of course they were all very complimentary. Then when she left, it got even worse for me. I could hear all of them talking about how good she was. And just then the person who had seated me in the first place came to get me. I wanted to ask if I could come back later for my audition so I could pull myself together, but I didn't. I got up on stage. I sang. I was pitchy. Then I read with the fantastic Tim Curry. I thought I was much too loud. When it all ended no compliments were given, only a hearty handshake, a thank-you, and a polite good-bye. Well, the rest is show biz history. And really, can you imagine anyone else playing that role of Janet? *Damn it!*

Young Frankenstein: Madeline Kahn was going to play the part of Elizabeth Lavenza, but had a conflict with another film she was supposed to do and so I was called in to read with Gene Wilder for Mel Brooks. I had the best darn time! It was such a funny script. And I had the part for a New York minute, until Madeline's schedule was rearranged so she could be in both movies. And honestly, could you ever envision anyone else playing that role but her?

Mack and Mabel: Gower Champion was directing this musical. I actually got up on stage at the Ahmanson Theatre in Downtown Los Angeles and sang for him. I got through my first song, "On the Radio" and from out in the darkness I heard, "Cindy, do you have another song?"

"Yes," I said.

I sang "Rubber Ducky." When I finished, I started off the stage and Mr. Champion said, "Wait! Stop!"

I stopped at the apron of the stage and he came up and looked at me and said, "I just wanted to get an up-close look at you." He

Shirley, I Jest!

gazed at me intensely and after a few seconds said, "You are a raw talent!"

I was thrilled that Gower Champion had taken the time to acknowledge me as a talent, raw or otherwise. The part of Mabel Normand went to Bernadette Peters just because *she* can sing and dance!

Star Wars: George Lucas sent me the script and wanted me to screen test for the role of Princess Leia. Now what you have to remember is that this was before *Star Wars*! There was no point of reference. Earlier, I had been to George's house with some of the *American Graffiti* cast when he was writing it. I remember him talking about it and how he had gotten the idea of Chewbacca by seeing his wife pull up in the driveway with their dog, Indiana, sitting in the passenger seat next to her. He thought Indiana looked like her copilot. So there you go. Years later, I would think once again "what a genius," when Sean Connery says to Harrison Ford in *Indiana Jones*, "You were named after the dog."

Back to Princess Leia. After I read the script, I wondered how I was going to handle all of those words of very, very far off foreign references. They did not flow easily off my tongue, but I wanted this part. I memorized as best as I could. Coincidentally I screen tested with Frederic Forrest, who was also in *The Conversation*. It was a rude awakening to realize just how bad I was at screen testing. Even so, I held out hope that George would see past all my faltering with the lines and know that when it came down to it, I'd be perfect.

A week later I had a dream: I was looking at a girl, younger than myself. I knew she was younger because in my dream she was playing with dolls. George was also in the dream, arms folded, one hand up to his chin, rubbing it in deep contemplation, watching the young girl. He turned from watching her and looked over at me, then back to the girl. When I woke up, I knew I wasn't getting the part.

Sure enough, he cast Carrie Fisher, who is younger than me. I was disappointed and wished I had tried harder in the screen test. But really, can you imagine anyone but Carrie playing Princess Leia?

First Nudie Musical: I did however, get the romantic lead in my friend Bruce Kimmel's musical film extravaganza, *The First Nudie Musical.* Bruce was my friend from LACC days and told me an idea he had for "sending up" X-rated movies by writing a low-budget musical about a film studio that is on the verge of collapse. The only way they can bail themselves out is by making X-rated films in the hopes of making enough money to then be legit again. Bruce's initial idea, I thought, was so clever. He wanted to shoot it on 8 mm and blow it up so it would have that grainy "adult film" look. Bruce was masterful at writing the musical numbers as well as the dialogue.

I felt like it was going to be a blast, and I gave no thought to what people might think. It was risqué, but all in good fun. The only thing I had a real problem with was the nudity. There was too much of it. And I told Bruce how I felt. But being the consummate artist that he was, he said he wanted all the nudity to stay in. Many of our friends from college were in it, including Lynne. She had a scene with Ron Howard. They are sitting outside the audition room with a group of people waiting their turn to go in. Ron turns to Lynne and asks, "Is this SAG?"

I asked him how he made the decision to do it. Ron said he was interested in low-budget filmmaking and he wanted to be a part of it. (The film came out right after the first season of *Laverne*

& Shirley. I was given the moniker of "Little Miss Filth Mouth" in *People* magazine under a delightful picture of me as Shirley.)

Not much had changed, I was pretty much broke and I was now living in an apartment in Hollywood that was basically empty except for a couch, a bed, two lamps, a Bible, and a box of kittens that needed homes! Aside from *The Tonight Show* and some other talk shows, nothing was on the horizon. The thought of going back to waiting tables crossed my mind. The problem was I had become too recognizable from *American Graffiti*. To wait tables in L.A. could prove to be humiliating. I thought about moving out of state where I might not be known, at least I would be far away from my peers.

And then one day out of the blue, I got a call from Francis Coppola's office asking if I'd be interested in writing for a bicentennial spoof he was producing called *My Country 'Tis of Thee*. The premise of the movie was the history of America from its discovery through modern times done in sketches and music. It would be released in 1976 to coordinate with our American bicentennial. The pay was less than desirable, but might be enough to keep me in town for a little while longer. They were hiring two-person writing teams and wanted to pair me up with Penny Marshall. I didn't know Penny very well. We were both represented by Compass Management, but had never met until a very memorable double date!

I had been invited to the Coconut Grove to see Liza Minnelli perform with Little Richard as the opening act. My date and I were doubling with Rob Reiner and Penny. The first time we actually met was in our seats at the Coconut Grove, seconds before the curtain went up, because my date and I arrived late. And during the performance Penny and I never exchanged words

Raw Talent

because we weren't sitting next to each other. When the show was over, we were all invited backstage to meet Liza. I was thrilled! As we walked backstage, Penny and I fell behind our dates as they walked ahead of us. To get to Liza's dressing room, we had to go through Little Richard's dressing room. As Penny and I started to cross through his room, he abruptly stopped us by putting his leg across the doorway.

We stopped. He said, "You two! I want to bless you two." Penny and I immediately bowed our heads and Little Richard proceeded to bless us, asking the Lord for his protection, along with happiness and success. When he was finished he shouted, "Amen!"

Then Penny and I shouted, "Amen!" And "the Reverend Penniman" smiled and nodded to us. We returned the gesture, smiling and nodding, and then went on our way. Years later Penny and I discussed this experience and we had two thoughts about it. Number one: we never told him how fantastic he was that night; and number two: we would always attribute much of our success with *Laverne & Shirley* to Little Richard's blessing.

By now Penny and I were on a writing team along with Steve Martin, Harry Shearer, Martin Mull, Marty Nadler, and Carl Gottlieb, who would be acting as producer/head writer. Penny and I trotted over to Samuel Goldwyn Studios to meet with Carl Gottlieb and the other writers. Everyone was given the assignment of "The Pilgrims Coming to America" and how they managed the journey.

We went into our nice office for the first time. Inside was a beautiful maple desk with a big leather chair behind it and a smaller chair in front of the desk. A couch and an end table with a phone on it sat against the wall. Penny immediately took the big chair behind the desk. That left me with the smaller chair in front of the desk. We started writing the first assignment, the one everybody had to take a crack at, "The Pilgrims Coming to America."

Penny and I thought, *What if we treat it like a concert?* It might be funny if everyone had to buy a ticket for passage to the "New World" on the *Mayflower*. And what if our character gets up to the window just as the last ticket was sold to the guy in front of him? The performance is sold out! Instead of scalpers, what if there's a guy selling passage to the New World on a giant catapult that is set up on the docks next to the *Mayflower*?

We had this poor guy buy a ticket and climb aboard with his luggage. Everyone taunts him and laughs at him. The guy running the catapult whispers in his ear: *Don't let them get to ya, you'll be havin' the last laugh.* With that, he cuts the ropes and *whoosh* off he goes just as the *Mayflower* sets sail. Our joke was that everyone on the *Mayflower* argues over who will be the first to set foot in the New World. And then, just as they reach land and the guy who won the honor is about to set his foot down, *whoosh* our catapult guy lands on Plymouth Rock beating him out, baggage and all!

Well, *we* thought the idea was funny! We wrote the sketch and turned it in to Carl. Carl weighed it. He had scales on his desk and as a joke he would actually weigh each person's written assignment. We thought that was funny too.

Our next assignment was "The Salem Witch Trials." We wrote a joke about a guy being accused of witchery because he continually keeps his hands in his pockets. Penny and I needed to come up with why he kept his hands in his pockets. We talked it out. I played the guy saying, "I agree. I do always keep my hands in my pockets. But I cannot be accused of witchery because—."

I looked at Penny. She responded, "I have paper hands."

Raw Talent

We both burst out laughing! We had no idea what it meant, but we thought it was funny. (Maybe we'd been listening to too much *Monty Python*.) Then we had a German shepard accused of being a witch. When the judge asks the courtroom, "Why is this dog in this court? Why is he charged of witchery, what is his offense?"

The dog screams: "I am not a witch, I denounce these proceedings. I am innocent of any evil doing!" We were having so much fun creating together. We both often thought in cartoon images when we were writing.

After "The Salem Witch Trials," Carl moved us on to "The U.S. Patent Office." We approached this using all the inventions of that era that were brought into the office to be patented. And when we got to Robert Fulton and his steamboat, Penny suggested that Fulton be our main character frantically trying to get the officials down to the river so they could see his invention. We were working on this sketch one day when the phone rang. Penny answered it.

She listened for a minute and then turned to me, holding the phone out, and said, "It's Garry. He wants to talk to you."

I got on the phone and Garry Marshall said, "Cindy, I was just asking Penny if you girls want to come and do a *Happy Days* episode. I've got these parts, Laverne and Shirley, girls who date the fleet. They're friends of Fonzie's, and he sets Richie and himself up on a double date with them. It'd be great if you and Penny could take a week off and come over to do the show."

Sounded like fun to me. I secretly thought, *I could use the money!* Penny agreed and Carl let us go for the week. Monday morning we left our day jobs and headed to Paramount. Penny and I talked about what our characters would do. When we made our entrance for the first rehearsal, we were chewing gum, smoking cigarettes, and adjusting our bras. We looked around for Richie and Fonzie, flicked our cigarettes across the room and began taking pin curls out of each other's hair while arguing back and forth with each other under our breath.

Jerry Paris, who was directing started screaming at us: "Stop! Stop! You can't do that. You can't *smoke* on family hour and all that other stuff. What do you think you're doing, a spinoff?"

Penny and I were slightly taken aback. Who knew about family hour? Neither of us had seen many *Happy Days* episodes and what the heck was a spinoff? We substituted gum for cigarettes, brought the tone down a little, but still arguing; still fixing each other's hair. We managed to make it just as much fun. I got to accidentally punch "Richie" and Penny got to kiss "The Fonz." Then it was over. We went back to our day jobs. We were in our office finishing up our "U.S. Patent Office" sketch with Fulton forming a conga line to take everyone down to the river to see his steam engine.

The phone rang, and it was Marty Nadler. He told us that everyone loved our *Happy Days* episode. They liked it so much that they wanted to do a spinoff, which meant Penny and I would have our own show. At this point it was just a big rumor. Life went on in our little office without mention of the word "spinoff" from anyone else. A week later, Carl gave us the assignment of "Sutter's Mill." However, I found myself alone. I hadn't seen or heard from Penny for a couple of days. I simply couldn't find her and we had this new assignment to write. I couldn't get her on the phone and when I came into the office in the morning she wasn't there. And "Sutter's Mill" was due, one way or the other. I researched "Sutter's Mill" and promptly started writing.

In the meantime I'd heard that Penny was writing with someone else. I was very confused. I went to Carl and asked him if he would hire my friend, Ed Begley Jr., as my writing partner. He said he couldn't do that because of the budget. I had to finish the assignment. Ed helped me write it anyway, giving me notes and suggestions while I sat in the office and typed it up. My plan was to finish it, turn it in, and quit. Impulsively, I quit first, telling Carl that I would finish up "Sutter's Mill" before I left. I started thinking about moving out of state again. I would have just enough money to do it.

Pat McQueeney, my manager at Compass, called and said Garry had called her and ABC was very interested in spinning the two characters of "Laverne and Shirley" off into a show of its own. Lowell Ganz, Mark Rothman, and Garry were writing a fifteen-minute presentation scene to shoot for the network. I told Pat I couldn't think about it because I had a writing deadline. I also told her I was thinking seriously about moving out of town.

"What on earth for?" she asked. She tried her best to argue with me telling me this could be a great opportunity—a show of my own! It could free me financially. She begged me to think about it, but told me not to take too long because Garry needed an answer about the presentation scene.

Honestly, looking back on it now, I'm not sure, but I might have been in some sort of depression. Before all of this started I had been on a two-year upswing in my career and then the floor seemed to drop out from under me. I was disappointed in myself and despondent. I wanted to get the heck out of Dodge. I felt a little bit let down by show business, and more let down and hurt by Penny, who remained missing in action. The idea of waiting tables anonymously gave me great comfort. Still, I continued alone, finishing my last writing assignment.

My manager called me day and night. My agent called me day and night. I started getting the feeling that this was a big deal. Pat said that the offer had been increased. It would be a four-show guarantee, which would mean a huge sum of money for me. I told her my reluctance was partially because Penny had disappeared on me and I couldn't discuss any of this with her. Pat told me to call her. I told Pat I had called her until I was blue in the face.

"Well, call her again, because you can't afford to lose this show and they're going to test other people."

I sat in front of my typewriter thinking of what to do. The fact that Penny had disappeared obviously affected me, but was it insurmountable? I mean, what if she had a great excuse? And did I really want to wait tables in another state? If there was a possibility I could make money here on the four shows that were being offered, wouldn't that be the smart thing to do? I looked down at my typewriter realizing I was only a few lines away from finishing my writing. I began to type when *Bang!* The office door flew open. It was Penny. I kept typing. The conversation went something like this:

"Hi!"

"Hi!"

Silence.

"So, are you gonna do the show?" she asked.

"I'm not really sure," I said.

"Why not?" she asked.

"I can't think about it. I'm finishing 'Sutter's Mill.'"

"Oh," she said sheepishly.

I thought, *Now's the time, Cindy, hit her with it. Say it! Where the hell have you been?* But I couldn't ask her. I didn't want to. I didn't want to put her on the spot.

"Are you gonna think about it?" she asked.

"Maybe."

Raw Talent

"Okay, but don't think too long, cause they're testing other people."

"So I've heard."

"Okay, so I'll see ya."

"See ya."

"Bye!" and with that she left.

We never spoke of it again. And many tales have been told as to why I didn't jump at the chance, in the beginning, of doing the show. But Penny's absence was the major reason.

I finished my writing, called Pat, and said, "I'll do it."

SEVEN

The Big Show

Penny and I snuck onto soundstage 20 at Paramount Studios. We wanted to look at the *Laverne & Shirley* set that had just been built and decorated. We were very excited! The next day we would begin rehearsals after having a table read of the first episode script with the writing staff, producers, and entire cast including guest actors. Up until now we had been appearing on *Happy Days* to establish the characters for *Laverne & Shirley* as local girls and friends of "The Fonz."

When we opened the heavy soundstage door and stepped onto the huge stage, the lights were on. No one else was around, not a soul but us! A soundstage is enormous, like a warehouse. There is usually more than one set housed within the building. For instance, on the *Laverne & Shirley* soundstage there were three sets. Laverne and Shirley's basement apartment, the Pizza Bowl set, and one other called a "swing-set." The swing-set is a space on the stage that can be used to build whatever is needed for that week's show. For instance, the swing-set for our first show was a dining area in a mansion for a gala dinner that Laverne and Shirley attended. In the "Fabian" episode it was his hotel suite and the ledge outside his window.

The show was to be shot with three cameras in front of a live studio audience seated on bleachers. Above the bleachers were the sound booth and the panel where the camera coordinator sat. Through headsets, he gave directions to each of the camera crew. The cameras were on wheels and pushed around by a "Dolly Grip" with the camera operator perched on a seat watching the action through the camera lens. A focus puller traveled with the camera to make sure the shot was clear. None of this was easy on our show because we were constantly moving like a slalom team. A lot of our camera crew had previously worked on *I Love Lucy* where this method had been perfected.

Penny and I walked backstage first. The dressing rooms, hair, makeup, and wardrobe were set up. We went onto the stage entering through Laverne and Shirley's front door. We couldn't believe our eyes! The apartment was beautiful: Wall-to-wall carpeting, cherrywood furniture, a fancy sofa, porcelain knickknacks, and expensive-looking wall hangings. We were stunned. In the pilot episode on *Happy Days* the nicest thing about our apartment was the kitchen sink and *that* was in the living room! What happened? This set was the exact opposite of what *Laverne & Shirley* was all about. It didn't take us long to decide what to do.

We split up! I drove to my mother's house in Reseda while Penny drove to her house in Encino. We gathered everything we thought would represent Laverne and Shirley's economic lack of status! I gathered my old, worn-out hooded coat from junior high, my high school albums, and pictures from my bedroom wall, stuffed animals, old movie magazines, clothes and stacks of newspapers my mother was saving for some ungodly reason. Penny was doing the same.

We met back on the soundstage and went to work. We took all the wall hangings down and hid them. We did the same with the porcelain knickknacks and the Queen Anne furniture. Penny brought a hammer and nails, her old forty-five record collection (a few of those went up on the walls), framed pictures, and old doilies my grandmother had crocheted. We started replacing the wall hangings with our own personal things. We hung all of the old clothing we brought in the entryway closet on the landing. We took the pristine magazines that sat on the pristine coffee table (nothing could be done right now about the coffee table) and replaced them with my mother's dog-eared movie magazines. We scattered various items that would read "old" on camera around the apartment. We placed a stack of old newspapers in front of the landing. We hid as many pieces of small furniture as we could in our dressing rooms. No one came onto the stage while we were up to our covert mission. We discussed the carpet and how we couldn't pull it up by ourselves. The set certainly wasn't 100 percent of what we imagined or wanted it to be, but it was certainly better than when we started. We would deal with the rest in the morning.

Well, morning came and all hell broke loose! The carpenters, set-dressers, and producers were upset. Garry came down. Everyone was standing on the stage commenting on our handiwork and not in a good way! We stated our case pointing out that Laverne and Shirley were blue-collar workers and would never be able to afford the furnishings in the apartment the way it had been decorated, let alone new wall-to-wall carpeting. Luxury defeated the purpose of the comedy. For this show to ring true, we needed to be girls that had to borrow folding chairs and found their sofa at the Goodwill, lugging it back to their apartment themselves. We needed to be barely above the poverty line. We needed to be hand-me-down girls who sometimes couldn't make the rent. The wolf always had to be nipping at our heels. We needed to be relatable to everyone. We got our way. And the carpet came up!

Our cast was great, innately funny, and we were natural foils for each other. David Lander and Michael McKean (Lenny and Squiggy) were cast due to Garry saying one day, "Laverne and Shirley need friends, people their age that maybe they went to high school with who were a rung or two lower on the mental and life skills ladder than them." Penny knew David and Michael from *The Credibility Gap*, which was a satirical political radio show. David and Michael had a routine they performed with two characters, "Lenny and Anthony." Penny threw a party, invited Garry, and had David and Michael perform "Lenny and Anthony." Garry hired them for the show. They changed the name "Anthony" to "Squiggy" and we were off to the races.

Eddie Mecca was cast as "Carmine" after he screen-tested. Eddie had been nominated for a Tony for Best Actor in *The Lieutenant* on Broadway. Aside from being a brilliant singer, dancer, and comedian, he is a fine dramatic actor. Phil Foster, a great stand-up comic, played Laverne's father and proprietor of the Pizza Bowl.

And then there was the sweetest, loveliest, ever-so-talented Betty Garrett. Betty was cast later in the series because the producers hadn't created the character of our landlady, Mrs. Babbish yet. Carole Ita White played our nemesis, Rosie Greenbaum, perfectly. When *Laverne & Shirley* move to California, Penny and

The Big Show

I referred to it as the unfortunate move to Burbank. We argued vehemently with Garry about the change and we lost. However, it did have its plusses. The first being the addition of the character of Rhonda, our next-door neighbor, played impeccably by Leslie Easterbrook. And then there was the ever-so-handsome Ed Marinaro who played the ever-so-handsome stunt man, Sonny.

Penny, David, Michael, Eddie, and Phil all had New York accents. Even Henry Winkler, "The Fonz," had one when he did a few episodes. Of course their accents were natural, because they all came from New York. But my thought was that if I didn't have an accent like theirs I'd stick out like a sore thumb. I adopted one for Shirley, and it was awful! I spoke with it through the first thirteen shows until one day Garry Marshall came down to the stage and sat me down.

He said something like, "It's about your accent."

"Is it awful?" I asked.

Garry said, "Yeah, pretty much so. Why don't you lose it?"

I was so grateful and relieved because I could hear it each week in the show and it made me cringe. I returned to my natural Texas/Valley Girl blended accent.

For the first season, the scripts always included physical comedy bits for Laverne, but not for Shirley. I spoke up saying I could do physical comedy, and pleaded with the writers and producers to give me the chance. My pleas fell on deaf ears and the scripts kept being written in the same manner. I had had such fun in the pilot episode where Shirley was more physical in nature; like accidentally punching Richie. But that physicality seemed lost as we went on into the first season. I longed for Shirley to have physical things to do so I continued my lobbying. Finally one day Garry came down to the set and told me he was writing a physical bit for me to see how I did. When the script came in, I was so happy! Laverne has a vacuum cleaner hose stuck to her mouth and can't get it off by herself. Shirley helps her. I had a lot of fun inventing ways to pull and twist that hose off of her mouth. The powers that be liked it because from then on, they wrote physical comedy for both of us.

Penny and I had a simple litmus test for comedy. If it didn't make us laugh, it probably wouldn't make the audience laugh; both in the studio and at home. So whatever it was, we had to laugh at it or we'd try something else until we did! And if it was a line or a part in the show that just "laid there," we did our best to pep it up. Usually all this doctoring up occurred during rehearsals. We'd give our notes after the table read each week, but didn't really know what was funny and what wasn't until we were on our feet and started putting movement with the lines.

Many times we'd take it upon ourselves to change lines. You can imagine how this ticked off the producers and writing staff. Sometimes Penny and I ticked each other off as well when we didn't agree on something. But I truly believe if we hadn't gone through what could be termed as chaos, we never would have had the show we had. Any time we stepped out on that stage together we were 100 percent in-sync. Whatever was going on off-stage evaporated when we got in front of our audience because we were of one mind and that was to entertain and make people laugh out loud.

Our premier show had an audience of almost thirty-six million viewers and we became an overnight hit! Garry came down to the stage with the news. Once again, just as with the talk of a spinoff, Penny and I did not immediately understand what this meant. We kept on working. We worked so hard there was no time for anything social. It was work and home, work and home.

The Big Show

There was no time for the outside world. Any function related to show business was usually something that took place on the Paramount lot.

One time they asked us to present at the *People's Choice Awards*. We said we were sorry but we were working and couldn't leave the set, get dressed, and into hair and makeup in time. The producers of the show told us not to worry, we could come straight from work with no need to get dressed up. Penny and I mulled it over. We would have to arrive at five thirty for the presentation. No way could we dress up. We turned it down. We were in the middle of putting together a huge physical scene and couldn't leave the rehearsal. They begged, and word came from Paramount that it would be good PR for the show if there were any way we could make it. In our rehearsal clothes (usually jeans, sweatshirts, and tennis shoes) we dutifully went. Standing backstage we saw that everyone was dressed to the nines, except us of course. We didn't let it get to us as we went out and presented. In the car on our way back to the studio, Penny made the observation that it was the *People's Choice Awards* and we were supposed to be a number-one show. Why hadn't we won a *People's Choice Award*? I couldn't answer. Maybe we were popular but not *that* popular, or maybe the people we were popular with didn't bother to vote. It wasn't a case of sour grapes. It was more of a curiosity.

One day toward the end of the first season I noticed a headline in the *Wall Street Journal* that someone had left on the stage. It read something like, "*Laverne & Shirley* Help Send ABC Stocks through the Roof!" I called Penny over. We both stood there taking in the words, reading them over and over.

Both Penny and I still thought in "cartoon" terms when it came to comedy. For instance, we would come up with "bits" to try during rehearsal and then stage them. We learned early on that life in the cartoon world doesn't always play out the way you imagine when it comes to life on earth.

In one of our first episodes, Laverne and Shirley are hosting a lingerie party in their living room. Shirley gives the description of the garment Laverne is supposed to model, it's a leopard teddy. The script called for her to swing in on a rope. During rehearsals, and thinking like a cartoon, we decided Penny would swing all the way across the room and then slam into the living room wall and slowly slide down (like Daffy Duck). We only "marked it" in rehearsal, which means she didn't actually climb onto the rope and swing across the room. We just said, *OK, I say this, you do that and you hit the wall and slide down.*

We used this format often to save our energy for the live show with the evening audience. When we actually performed it and Penny swung on the rope across the room, modeling her leopard ensemble, she hit the wall with "real-world force." And instead of sliding down the wall slowly, like Daffy Duck as we had imagined, she fell to the floor in a heap like Newton's apple! We had to stop filming. She had her ankle bandaged and we continued with the show.

In these days of TV, the networks were assigning censors for their "family hour" primetime shows. Their censors would attend the read-through as well as the run-through each week to ensure "moral content." Our censor was a born-again Christian. He was a great guy, but very strict, which turned out to work in our favor. The writers and the cast were forced to be more creative. An example is vo-de-oh-doh, which said it all. When Shirley had to talk about sex in any way, she would use the term vo-de-oh-doh and that became universally recognizable, and forever associated with the show. Having a censor didn't stop us, we were even more inventive and creative. Penny and I didn't kid ourselves. We knew we weren't the greatest show in the history of television. But every now and then, as a cast and as a show, we'd have a moment that was worthy of greatness.

On one show we had a scene where we were spring cleaning. It was an afternoon run-through for the writers and producers. I was supposed to be cleaning under my bed and yell to Laverne, "We've got dust bunnies the size of grapefruit under here!" I forgot the line and improvised, pulling out a stuffed black cat that our prop man, Rennie, had been keeping under there among other props. I looked it over and said, "Oh, look who I found, Laverne. It's Boo Boo Kitty!"

The scene continued and I didn't think about it until Boo Boo Kitty turned up in the next week's show and then became a mainstay character. The reason I had called this precious stuffed animal Boo Boo Kitty was because my mother had a cat we called Boo Boo Kitty, and we all loved her so much. She, unlike Shirley's Boo Boo Kitty, was black and white with beautiful green eyes. Shirley's Boo Boo was all black with one plastic diamond-shaped red eye and I always thought of it as a "he." My mother had two other cats that my sister and I had "given" her because she had a yard. They were named Charlotte and Simone. One day she received a notice from Animal Control that anyone having more than two cats would be fined. She called me to tell me this, but said not to worry because Boo Boo lived mostly across the street in the neighbor's tree.

There was one problem with Boo Boo Kitty, the actor. Rennie, the prop master, couldn't find a double. And since the writers were coming up with shows that included him, we needed a second one

Shirley, I Jest!

just in case anything was to happen to our original. He searched high and low and never found a match, and Boo Boo Kitty was ceremoniously locked away each night after the show. Rennie sweated bullets protecting the precious commodity like a mother bear would her cub. Over the years the search continued with no luck.

Then one day, years after the show had ended, I was at an autograph convention when two ladies came sauntering up to me, each holding a Boo Boo Kitty. I couldn't believe my eyes. I told them the story of the search and asked them where on earth they got them. They told me that they were attached to pajama bags that were sold at JC Penney in the 1960s. I asked if I could buy one from them and their answer was a polite but definite "no."

They loved their Boo Boo Kitties just like I did.

EIGHT

The Mirthful Mouse

The audience at the L.A. Improv had grown more than restless. They were actually trying to stop me from going on stage. Someone even reached out and tried to grab my arm, to hold me back, but I kept going.

A girl shouted at me, "Sit down, this guy's dangerous!"

She was referring to the ever-obnoxious Tony Clifton who was on stage challenging me: "Come on, lady. Be a man! Come up here and let's settle this face-to-face!"

Truth be known, I wanted to make a hasty retreat and hightail it back to my apartment and hide under the coffee table, but it was too late for that. I had to stay committed. I shouted back in a horrible French accent (as we had rehearsed): "You are a repulsive and eedious leetle man!"

"Shut up and sit down," another person from the audience barked at me.

But I soldiered on, inching my way onto the stage against massive audience protest. Obviously they weren't getting it. I started wondering how I had let Andy Kaufman talk me into this. Did I really believe it would be funny and make people laugh? At this

Shirley, I Jest!

moment in time all we were accomplishing was agitating the ten o'clock audience at the Improv.

It all started about a year earlier, on practically the very same spot; it was the second season of *Laverne & Shirley*. Penny and I had been asked by the Improv if we would come to the club and have our picture taken for Budd Friedman, the club's owner. Penny and I considered it a great compliment to have our picture taken with him. The photo would hang on the celebrity wall of the club. We posed for the picture and mingled for a while. I was tired and wanted to get home. I said my good-byes and as I was going out the front door onto Melrose Avenue, I saw a lone figure standing on the sidewalk. I recognized him immediately—it was Andy Kauffman. It would have been pretty hard for me *not* to recognize him. I was a *huge* fan. And he was wearing the same ill-fitting sports jacket he wore on *Saturday Night Live*! I went up to him to introduce myself.

"Hi!" I said. "I'm Cindy!"

"Hi, I'm Andy!"

"I know, I love you!" I blurted out impulsively.

"I mean I love how you think, your timing. You make me laugh out loud! And I have a greater appreciation of Elvis Presley because of you!"

He looked at me, puzzled, blinked his sparkly brown eyes, and said, "Thank you," and asked me for a ride home. So began my friendship and adventures with Andy Kauffman!

Andy lived in an apartment in Hollywood. He was a Buddhist, a strict vegetarian, and didn't drive. On occasion we would go to my mother's house in Reseda for dinner. Even though her health doctrine included the belief that everybody needed red meat at

The Mirthful Mouse

least once a week, she was more than happy to cook him a vegetarian dinner.

Carol lived with my mother at this time and she was also a big fan of Andy's. She was especially fond of his "Mighty Mouse" because when she was a little girl she was in love with Mighty Mouse and determined to marry him! I was to be her maid of honor.

Andy meditated on the twenty-five-minute drive to Reseda. If he wasn't done with his meditation by the time we arrived, I would simply leave him in the car and go inside. When he was finished he would come inside and join my mother, my sister, and me. The first time this occurred my mother asked where he was. I told her he was in the car finishing his meditation. My mother, my sister, and I went to the front window that looked out over the driveway and watched him for a minute. The front porch light cast an almost angelic glow on him as he sat there eyes closed, floating in some other world.

"I hope he hurries," my mother lamented. "I can't keep his brown rice and tofu warm forever!"

We always had great fun when Andy came over. He taught us parlor games, we'd have sing-alongs, and he even tried to get my mother to participate. He was like a great camp counselor, leading us in song, games, and festivities. I wish my father would have been alive. He would have enjoyed him so much.

We spent a Christmas at my mother's. I gave everybody hoodies as Christmas presents. Andy really liked his hoodie; at times he substituted it for his ill-fitting sports jacket! He even wore it on *Saturday Night Live.*

Rehearsals and shooting on *Laverne & Shirley* were consuming all of my time. My free time was very limited. Andy didn't understand the grueling schedule and pressure I was under. This was before he started playing Latka on *Taxi*. One time he had caught a cold and asked me to grocery shop for him, which I did. On my way to the studio, I dropped off the bag of groceries at his apartment. Standing at his door, he asked me if I would come back later to drive him to pick up his prescription. I told him I couldn't because rehearsal was going to run late. He pitched a little fit telling me he didn't understand why I had to be at work so much. I tried my best to explain, but it fell on deaf ears. I was going to be late! I had to rush, leaving him there, wearing his hoodie over his pajamas, Kleenex up to his nose in one hand, the grocery bag filled with bananas, vegetable soup, crackers, and juice in the other. He was not a happy camper when I left. Later when he was doing *Taxi* at Paramount, he came over to the *Laverne & Shirley* soundstage where I was rehearsing. He asked if he could speak to me for a minute.

I said, "Sure."

We stepped off to the side and he said, "Cindy, I want to apologize to you for that time I got upset with you for having to rush off to rehearsal. I understand now why you had to go, and how difficult it all is."

Laverne & Shirley was on hiatus and I found myself in New York. Andy was there as well taping *Saturday Night Live*. He called to say he was booked for the 10:00 p.m. set at Catch a Rising Star, a popular comedy club in Manhattan. He asked me if I would help him.

I didn't hesitate, I simply responded, "I would love to. What do you need me to do?"

He asked me if I could go-go dance. I said, "Yeah, sure, I can go-go dance. What do you need? The hitchhike? The jerk? The swim?"

The Mirthful Mouse

He said, "All of them! And when it's our turn to go on stage, you go as far up-stage as you can, keep your back to the audience, and your head down. And when I say to the audience, 'I suppose you want me to sing,' that'll be your cue to cross down-stage and stand to my left, slightly behind me. And when I start to sing, you start to go-go dance. OK?"

"OK!" *Oh, this is gonna be fun*, I thought! He didn't tell me anything else and I didn't ask. I didn't want to know. I wanted to be surprised! I was thrilled to perform with him.

We arrived at the club, which had about thirty people in the audience, all down front. Andy's popularity was not quite at a high point; he wasn't exactly a household name yet. When Andy was introduced and we went on stage, I noticed he had a book in his hand. There was only a smattering of applause. I could see this audience had been drinking—a lot! Their faces were red and shiny! I thought, *hmm, this could go south, fast.*

I took my place up-stage, back to the audience, head bowed. There's silence for a beat. Andy clears his throat. And then he begins to read. He begins reading *The Great Gatsby*. He reads in quiet tones with subdued passion. I'm thinking, *He's a very good actor!* He reads on, emphasizing the drama of the text. I start to hear grumbling from the audience. But Andy is not fazed. He continues. More grumbling. They're getting agitated and I'm sweating through my outfit! *He is pokin' the beehive now*, I thought!

A mantra of shouting begins.

"Get off the stage! Get off the stage!"

Undaunted, Andy reads on.

"Come on, man, really, get off the stage! Get off the stage!" Booing ensues.

Andy shouts back at them, "You people don't like literature?"

Shirley, I Jest!

"No!"

He slams the book closed. "OK," Andy says. "I suppose you want entertainment!"

"Yeah!"

"I suppose you want jokes!"

"Yeah!"

"I suppose you want me to sing!"

"Yeah!"

This is my cue. I cross downstage and stand behind Andy, slightly to his left. I get a look at the crowd that has settled down somewhat. I can't say they were ugly, but they weren't pretty! And yes, they were drunk! I'm thinking, *Here it comes, he's gonna sing, I'm gonna dance, and then let's get outta here.*

Andy begins to sing. He begins to sing the title song from the musical *Oklahoma!* What? I have no time to process this. I immediately start doing the jerk and move onto the twist, the hitchhike, and then the swim. Andy takes a stance with his chest puffed out, hands on hips and performs the song with the verve I'm certain Rodgers and Hammerstein had intended! The crowd is stymied! Silenced! Sort of like you would imagine a courtroom to be if someone shouts, *I did it, I did it! Ramon is innocent!*

Andy sang the entire song, and I used up all my best go-go moves. At one point I even did the backstroke. When it was over he bowed, I bowed. There was another smattering of applause, but mostly the audience was stunned. They didn't know what to make of it! And you know what, even though it was a thrill to perform with Andy, it would have been equally as thrilling for me to sit in that audience and be entertained by him.

Andy and his friend and writing partner, Bob Zmuda, were working on a new character, a nightclub entertainer named Tony

Clifton. Tony Clifton involved makeup, a phony nose, costuming, and a hideous chauvinistic attitude. Simply put, he was a rotten character all the way around. Andy loved playing him and could not be dissuaded, no matter who protested. One weekend Andy was performing a Sunday night set at the Improv in L.A. And he was going to have "Tony" perform. He was coming over to my house Friday night, and we were going to spend the weekend together just having fun. I've described this experience the best way I can.

At this point I had never seen the character of Tony Clifton, I'd only heard of him from Bob and Andy. Andy informs me that he's staying in character the *entire* weekend, so he'll be ready for the Sunday night show. I don't think too much about this until Bob drops him off. When I opened the door, the first thing I noticed was Bob sitting in his car, in the driveway waiting to see my reaction. I looked at Andy. He stood there gazing down at me looking like a member of the Rat Pack gone mad! The suit he was wearing was horrendous! He was carrying a briefcase and a cheap-looking garment bag. He had a malevolent look about him. I must have reacted to this in the way they intended, because Bob waved at me and laughed as he drove off!

Andy pushed me aside and said he needed a drink.

I said, "You don't drink and besides I don't have any liquor here."

He says, "Yeah, well next time, take care of that!"

He's speaking in a manner I had never heard before. He rattles off a list of things that will be required for his stay. He hands me the garment bag and demands that I press his other suit and hang it up so it will be ready for Sunday night. He's going so fast I can't catch up to him.

Shirley, I Jest!

I tell him, "Cut it out, Andy! I thought we were going to dinner and to see a movie?"

He asks me who Andy is and tells me, "I'm spending the weekend with you, baby, not this Andy!"

He informs me he doesn't want dinner and a movie, he wants to go somewhere where there are "women and booze!"

"Come on, Andy," I tell him. "I don't find any of this funny!"

He peers in my bedroom and asks me, "Where are *you* going to sleep?"

I warn him. "Andy, stop!"

He says, "Again, with this Andy, is that some jerk you're seeing on the side?"

"Stop it, Andy!"

"There's that name again." He continues marching around my apartment checking everything out. At one point he sees my cat, Chang, and insists he wants "that thing" kept in the bathroom, "so he can't look me in the eye!"

I tell him for the last time, "Cut. It. Out!" He chuckles at me. Now I've had it! I grab his hair at the temple and when I know I have a firm grip, I start pulling.

"I don't like doing this and I need you to stop immediately, whoever you are!"

He pinches my cheek. I pull his hair harder. My cat makes a mad dash for the bedroom to hide.

Andy won't break character and now he's laughing at me, mocking me in an odious manner.

"You women are all alike. You think you're strong, but you're not!"

"Really?"

The Mirthful Mouse

I yank his hair even harder pulling his head toward the floor. I get his head to the floor. He lets out a yelp, and starts laughing and finally breaks character.

"OK, OK, I give! Let go!"

"Really?" I ask, maintaining my grip.

"Really!" he says.

"I don't believe you."

"Believe me!"

"Prove it! Be Elvis!"

"OK! OK!" he says. I let go and without missing a beat he pops up, looks me in the eyes, and says, "Well, hello, little lady!"

An hour later Elvis and I went to dinner and saw a movie!

Before Andy, I never really appreciated Elvis Presley as much as other people did. When I was in junior high, a contest was held: Elvis Presley or Roy Orbison. *Who was the better singer*? I voted for Roy Orbison. Roy Orbison's voice made me feel, at thirteen, like I was living in a beautiful, romantic dream. But now, Andy made me understand. Somehow when Andy transformed into Elvis, I got it! I understood the majesty of Elvis Presley.

Andy told me one time he found himself in Las Vegas in an elevator with Elvis Presley. Elvis recognized him and said, "I understand you impersonate me!"

Andy said, "Yes I do!"

So Elvis asked Andy to do just that right there, impersonate him. I forget which song Andy told me he sang to Elvis as Elvis, but when he was done, Elvis told Andy, "Yeah! That's good! You're really good!"

Andy took that as a sincere compliment.

I'm not sure where this falls in the order of things, but I believe it was just around the time he started playing the character of

Shirley, I Jest!

Latka on *Taxi*. We were playing around, improvising. He started taunting me as Tony Clifton. I started shouting back at him, as an even-more obnoxious character. An in-your-face, brassy French woman! Anyone who has seen the first season of *Laverne & Shirley*, when I tried matching Penny's Bronx accent, knows I'm miserable at it. I don't have the ear for accents. I sounded like Maurice Chevalier hopped up on cold medication. It made us laugh. These two characters, going at it! Tony Clifton being challenged by this French woman! Of course, Andy wanted to try it out on a crowd.

We were going to do a late set at the Improv in L.A. I would sit in the audience. He would start his Tony Clifton routine and go on about how women were inferior and how they belonged in the kitchen. At this point I would start heckling him from the audience; shouting back how he was a hideous little man and how he should be ashamed of himself.

That brings us back to the beginning when the audience was trying to stop me from going on-stage. Even though he was on *Taxi* and I was on *Laverne & Shirley*, I realized no one recognized us. When I finally made it on-stage as we'd rehearsed, we slung insults at each other volleying back and forth, then getting slightly physical, with him gently smacking my face. The audience screamed in horror. I tried to deck him. We circled each other and then at one point, I stood on a chair we had "pre-set." I jumped on his back and he tried to throw me off. I shouted a few more insults, he shouted back and managed to "pretend-fling" me off. I ran off-stage and in my bad French accent screamed, "Yoo muzzure fuk-kah!!" Andy continued his routine as Tony, while I stood off-stage. I felt someone breathing on my neck. I turned around and it was Budd Friedman, the Improv's owner, who usually loves Andy and me. He glared at me and waited until Andy got off-stage.

The Mirthful Mouse

"What was that, what do you two think you were doing out there?" Budd asked.

Andy tried to explain that it was a bit he was trying out as Tony Clifton, a new character he was developing. Budd informed us both that it was awful and we can't be doing that kind of material in the club. He asked us to leave.

We found ourselves out on the sidewalk on Melrose Avenue in front of the Improv right where we began on the night we first met. The circle was complete.

Except this time I was speechless in my humiliation. Andy was laughing, he thought it was great. I told him he was crazy and he should never try that character again. I gave him a ride home, and because of our hectic TV schedules we wouldn't see each other for a while. But when we did, we would make up in spades for fumbling the comedy football that night at the Improv.

In 1979, Andy called me and asked if I'd be on his TV special, titled *Andy's Funhouse*.

"Well, yes!" I said.

I had finally recovered from our debacle at the Improv in L.A. Andy was working a few soundstages away from me on the Paramount lot on *Taxi* while I did *Laverne & Shirley*. He hadn't written the entire special yet, but he and Bob Zmuda had ideas. The special would be a talk show with Andy as the host sitting slightly elevated above his guests. Along with Howdy Doody, he wanted me to be one of his guests. We started throwing around ideas about what to talk about. I don't know whose idea it was, but Edward Albee's *The Zoo* story came up. Andy thought if he started off by asking me what I was up to I'd answer, "Well, I went to the zoo today."

Shirley, I Jest!

Then he would continue on prompting me into going through the entire monologue of the play which would end with me killing him. As he was dying, he'd cut to commercial. We, of course, thought it was hysterical. Bob and Andy ran it by the network and they flipped out. So instead they wrote an introduction for me that was something like, "She was in *American Graffiti, Travels with My Aunt,* and *The Conversation.* She is also a member of the prestigious Actors Studio. Ladies and gentlemen, please welcome Cindy *Laverne & Shirley* Williams!"

Then they had me come out to a podium with low lighting and read a poem about death. But the thing I had the most fun with was Andy insisting I was booked to sing "Mack the Knife" with the Rag Tag Band he had on the show. I told him I know nothing about this. I don't even know the lyrics! Andy talked over me, leading the audience in applauding me on and I was *forced* to sing. (Of course this was all rehearsed.) Purposefully I never rehearsed or learned the words. I had the most fun trying to sing the song, stopping when I didn't remember a line, and the band stopping with me. Andy would shout it out and the band would start up again. If I can remember, it did have a great flourish at the end or maybe I'm imagining that. Andy's TV special was a big hit with both the audience and the critics. I was proud of my friend!

The next time I saw Andy was one night during the filming of our show. Penny and I were dressed as cave women. We were standing on the stage off to the side watching a scene being shot. Andy came up between us and whispered these words: "Penny, Cindy, would you girls mud wrestle me at the Shrine on Friday night?"

Penny and I looked at each other, considered it, but had to tell him no, we'd be too tired from rehearsals. Andy said he'd make it easy on us. We still had to turn him down. Discussing it later, I told Penny that maybe we should have made the effort. I could see the funny picture in my head. It was pure Andy Kaufman!

The very last time I saw Andy he had arrived late to my house for a party. Most of the guests had left and we were in the process of cleaning up. He sat down on the couch with Carol. Harriet, the bartender, took me aside and, gesturing toward Andy, asked, "Is that Andy Kaufman over there?"

"Yes, it is!" I said.

"Do you think he'd wrestle me?" she asked.

"I'm pretty certain he would!"

"Will you ask him?"

I went over to him and said, "Andy, will you wrestle Harriet?"

Andy looked up. Harriet gave him a little wave and with that we all helped to clear the furniture from the center of my living room. Harriet removed her bartender's vest and belt. Andy took off his jacket and handed it to Carol. They circled each other and then it was a melee of arms grabbing waists, quasi-chokeholds, and a little tripping.

"Cindy, get your camera!" Carol shouted. "Take a picture!"

I did and it was a good one. I'm sad to say I can't find the picture to put in this book. Harriet had Andy in some sort of hold. He was going pale.

I thought, *she's good!*

Maybe Andy had finally underestimated his opponent.

NINE

————

The Adventures of Laverne and Shirley

Like many of the TV stars in those days, Penny and I were asked to record our own album, and we did "Laverne and Shirley Sing," which consisted of hits from the 1950s and '60s like *Chapel of Love*, *Da Do Ron Ron*, and *Sixteen Reasons*. One of our stops for the promotion of our album was Philadelphia to appear on *The Mike Douglas Show*. Then we were headed into New York where we would be staying for the next two weeks for more promotion and to be in the Macy's Thanksgiving Day Parade.

Instead of taking the train, a stretch limo was sent for us. The driver was a nice young man named Phil and this just happened to be his first day on the job. When he saw who he was driving he got very excited and told us what big fans he and his family were. Penny and I got into the car and settled in for the long drive from Philly to Manhattan.

We hadn't been in a limousine as large as this, ever! It had a bar, television, and couch. It also had a moon roof that let light in, but we couldn't find the switch to open it. I tried pushing on it with my hands, but it didn't budge. Penny tried pushing on it with her feet. It still wouldn't move. We asked Phil how it opened.

Shirley, I Jest!

He didn't know either. Not only was it Phil's first day, but Phil also didn't know Manhattan! He had a map, but by now it was dark. We had somehow managed to get ourselves into Central Park so he couldn't pull over and stop. We knew we needed to be on the other side of the park to get to the Sherry-Netherland Hotel where we were staying. Penny knew the city better than I did, and at some point told Phil to take a right. That took us onto a one-way street. The only problem was we were going in the wrong direction. We had just turned around when flashing lights came up behind us. It was the police. Phil pulled over obeying the voice on the loud speaker. Poor Phil! He was trembling.

"Oh boy," he said. "My first day and I'm going to get a ticket and tomorrow I'll be fired!"

Penny and I looked at each other. We flung the car door open, sank to our knees, clasped our hands together, and begged: "Please don't give Phil a ticket! It's his first day! It was our mistake!"

A huge spotlight from the police car hit us and from behind it an incredulous voice shouted, "Oh my God! It's Laverne and Shirley!"

Well, Phil didn't get a ticket and the nice policemen ushered our limo to the hotel! We thanked the officers, promised autographed pictures, and made sure Phil could find his way home. We offered him a room for the night, but he said he needed to get back to Philadelphia for his second day on the job. He thanked us many times over and we waved to him as he left, both of us hoping he would find his way.

The Sherry-Netherland Hotel on 5th Avenue and East 59th Street is an enchanting place. It has a small lobby with a beautiful, ornate marble floor, gorgeous chandeliers, and gracious staff. When you step into the lobby you get a sense of the wonderful people and things that have gone on there. They gave us beautiful accommodations. We each had a two-bedroom suite, and each one had a sound system with large speakers that sat on either side of the fireplace mantel. It was odd to me, but I guess since we were in town for our record promotion, Atlantic Records thought we might want to, I don't know, play our album for guests? My suite was on the twenty-second floor. (There's that number again!) I avoided looking out toward the park and the carriage horses standing in the cold. It has always made me sad. They seem so tired. Do they ever get to play?

The first day of promotion in New York we were taken out to Sam Goody Records in Paramus, New Jersey, to promote our album. We had been working so much that we honestly didn't realize just how popular the show was. We were literally mobbed. We were pushed to the back of the store by the crowd they let in the door. Penny and I had to stand up on a table and ask everyone to settle down so we could have our meet-and-greet. It was bedlam. We had to have security guards holding back the wave of *Laverne & Shirley* humanity! The frenzy had just begun. The next day we were in the Macy's Thanksgiving Day Parade.

During the parade our float stopped to let us off to lip-sync *Da Do Ron Ron*, which we chose because we thought it would be a crowd pleaser. We had just started the song when we saw the crowd break through the barriers and run toward us. Penny and I, still not used to our newfound popularity, looked behind us to see *who* it was they were rushing to see. Realizing it was us, we hastily hopped back up on the float to finish our song.

After the parade I went back to the hotel. Fans stood outside asking for autographs. It was all very flattering! Penny had gone off with some friends so I ordered Thanksgiving dinner for myself. Dinner had just been brought up when there was a knock at the door. I answered it to find John Belushi standing there. If I could describe this man to you I would tell you that I found him magical, and crazy as a hatter. I adored him, but what was he doing here? I asked him to come in. The waiter was still setting up my Thanksgiving table. John was eyeing it. The waiter was eyeing him. I asked him if he had had dinner yet. He said no. I asked him if he'd like me to order one for him. He said yes. I asked the waiter to please bring up another Thanksgiving dinner. And while we were waiting John started looking out the window.

The day before, I had been in Penny's suite when John showed up there. The three of us were having a good time chatting. Then we started discussing the sadness people feel around the holidays. Penny's sound system and speakers were on the mantel. I had brought my Electric Light Orchestra cassette tape with me and wanted to play them a cut from it explaining how uplifting it was to me. I put it on and we all started listening. It was pretty spectacular music. John walked over to the speakers putting one up to each ear as if they were headphones and nodding his head in time with the music.

He said, "Oh yeah. Yeah I'm gettin' it now. This is doin' it! This could change somebody's mood. It's changing mine right now."

And with that, he ran for the window. Penny and I leapt up in unison and ran after him each grabbing an arm just as he got to the window, which was wide open. We pulled him back. He was laughing. Now, we knew he wasn't going to fling himself off the twenty-third floor of the Sherry-Netherland. We knew it was all in good fun. And we also knew he ran full speed knowing darn well we'd catch up with him. I have to admit it was funny. Scary, but funny.

The Adventures of Laverne and Shirley

Finally, the waiter showed up with John's dinner and we sat down to eat. He put his napkin up to his face and pretended to sneeze endive out of his nose. It really made me laugh. When we were sitting there eating dinner, he looked at me and said something like, "I have to tell you something. I think my apartment is burning down."

"What? Your apartment is burning down?"

"Yeah, I'm not sure, but I think so."

"You think so?"

"Maybe I should go check on it."

"Maybe you should!"

"Yeah, you're right."

And with that, he took a dinner roll off the table, put it in his pocket, and left. I tried to call after him, "Wait! John, maybe we should call somebody!"

But he was already gone. I tried calling Penny, but couldn't get ahold of her. I never did find out if there was actually a fire.

I called home. I asked my mother if she had watched the parade. She had and of course loved our performance. My mother had become a one-woman booster club. She was now working at Bill White's Foods for Health in Van Nuys, dishing out healthy organic food. Bill White's was very popular with actors like Steve McQueen and Ali MacGraw, all kinds of celebrities came in. And I was happy to sign pictures as she dispensed health advice for her adoring friends and customers. This was her purpose-driven life and it made her happy, kept her healthy, and she reveled in it. One day a reporter came into Bill White's and asked my mother for an interview for a ladies' magazine. My mother, of course, was thrilled to participate. They even took a picture of her. Well, when the article came out, lo and behold it was not for a ladies'

Shirley, I Jest!

magazine as she had been told, it was for *The Enquirer* and the headline read: "Daughter Makes Millions While Mother Works as a Waitress."

It was accompanied by a picture of my mother in a waitress uniform holding a plate of food in each hand and smiling into what seemed to be a fish-eyed lens. My poor little mama, sucked in by a show business rag sheet. But you know what I hope? I hope the reporter did think long and hard about how she turned something that should have been upbeat into crap. My mother phoned the "reporter" not to give her a piece of her mind but to ask her why and how she could deceive her. My mother said she wanted her to think about it. The reporter had no answer except to say "I'm sorry, Frances." If that reporter had only asked, she would have known that I had tried many times to get her to stop working, and she turned my offer down every time. She loved her job and at this point in her life she had no intention of quitting. She also knew I would have given her anything her little ol' heart desired. All she had to do was ask!

In 1980, Penny and I were sent by Paramount to the TV Festival de Cannes. It's a once-a-year gathering of foreign distributers seeking to buy shows for programming in their country. We were the ambassadors for *Laverne & Shirley* and were scheduled to attend cocktail parties and dinners, hosting and meeting distributors. Paramount was hoping to sell the show to foreign markets.

Our plane was late arriving in Orly Airport in Paris and we were both in a pretty wretched state. Of course neither of us spoke French and making our connecting flight to Cannes was more than challenging. We had to gather our luggage and run like bats out of hell to catch the flight. We didn't understand any of the instructions

The Adventures of Laverne and Shirley

we were given. All we could figure out was that we had to hurry from one terminal to another with our luggage piled on one trolley. Penny pushed, I steered! It must have been a mile. We rounded one corner and lost our balance, careening into a wall, ping-ponging back, and trying to keep the luggage from falling. We sailed down one corridor after the next. We ran faster and faster. Finally we rounded one last bend and made it. Our luggage was checked. We now had to run to the gate and run we did! We were out of breath when we got there. The last few passengers were boarding. There was a table with boxes and bottles of wine. The people ahead of us each grabbed a box and a bottle. We did the same.

Everyone on the plane had skis and was dressed in winter attire. We took our seats at the back of the plane, which took off like a rocket and without much warning. People immediately started drinking wine and eating their lunches. We did the same. Neither of us drank, but halfway through the flight, when we were over the Alps, we hit major turbulence. Penny frantically lit a cigarette. I gulped down all of my wine. The turbulence never ended. We looked at each other, then at the passengers around us. In fact they were oblivious to the bumpy flight. It looked like a disco party in full swing. We shrugged our shoulders figuring everything was fine. We finished the wine. The landing was like the takeoff, fast and sudden. But we made it.

We were picked up and taken to one of the most beautiful places on earth as far as I'm concerned, the Hotel du Cap Eden-Roc in Antibes, France. It sits on the Mediterranean Sea. We were jet-lagged and exhausted. Our rooms were next door to each other and were beautiful. Each room provided a butler and a maid. They were situated in the hallway in little cubicles. Whenever we'd come in or go out of the room, they'd both stand at attention. They were each dressed impeccably. I commented to Penny that they were dressed better than we were.

Penny commented back, "Ugly Americans, Cin, we're ugly Americans!"

I told her to stop it. We were so exhausted, but we had to stay awake because we had a big business dinner that night. Even though it was cold, we decided to take a walk. The hotel is situated on the Mediterranean with a beautiful, lilac-trellised path that leads to the sea. It was spectacular. There was a hothouse where they grew the flowers that sat in large vases in the hotel, and fruits and vegetables for the restaurant. We were so tired we huddled together as we walked, keeping in step with each other.

At one point Penny lit a cigarette and the smoke was blown into my face by a nice little ocean breeze. There was no use asking her to put it out. I knew she wouldn't and anyway I didn't want to see her stomping it out among the lilac petals scattered about the ground. We kept in step, never missing a beat, and made it to the stone cliff that rose high above the water. We didn't stop. Gazing briefly at the crystal turquoise sea, we headed back. Penny lit another cigarette off the butt from the first one; a lovely picture of delicate charm. As we made our way back up the path to the hotel, still walking under the lilac-strewn trellis, I noticed up ahead what I thought to be a graveyard, only with small headstones.

"Look!" I said to Penny. "They have their own pet cemetery."

"What?" Penny said.

"Look!" I pointed. "They have their own cemetery where they bury their pets."

Penny glanced to the tiny headstones. "That's not a pet cemetery."

"What is it then? Look at the headstones, they're so small." We were getting closer to where the headstones were lined up.

The Adventures of Laverne and Shirley

"It's probably a place where they bury the help!" she said.

"The help? Don't be crazy!"

"Yeah, the help, the small help—the butlers, the maids that have worked here."

"I'm telling you it's a pet cemetery; the French love their animals."

"The French love their butlers and maids who die here too," she said, taking a final triumphant drag from her cigarette. We had arrived at one of the graves.

"Really," I said, reading a headstone to her.

"Au revoir mon petite Skippy?" I turned to her, "Skippy was the butler?"

She didn't care, she had gone on to light another cigarette.

That evening we were scheduled to have dinner with buyers at Le Grand Hotel in Cannes. We were wretched creatures by this time. We were among the living dead! We tried to dress up, but no matter what either of us put on, we always looked like we were wearing pajamas and slippers. When we walked out of our rooms to meet in the hallway, once again the butler and maid stood at attention in their cubicle. Again as we walked, Penny says, "Ugly Americans, Cin, we're ugly Americans!" Once again, I told her to shut up.

We arrived at the Le Grand Hotel in Cannes and were escorted into the ornate private dining room, complete with ceiling-to-floor beveled glass windows, French crystal chandeliers, and a long dining table that was set for about sixty people. Everywhere in the room there were exquisite flower arrangements set in crystal vases. Penny and I were alone in the room. Exhausted, we sat down at the table next to each other. A waiter came over and politely asked in English if we would like to order drinks. We each requested double espressos, laid our heads down in the beautiful Lalique dinner plates, and fell fast asleep.

We were awakened by a voice saying, "Penny! Cindy!"

When we raised our heads we saw Loretta Switt about thirty feet away smiling and sitting at the other end of the table. "Come here and sit with me," she said.

Penny said, "We're too exhausted, Loretta. We can't move!"

Our espressos had been placed in front of us. We started drinking them, hoping to come to. People started trickling in, buyers and Paramount representatives. Soon we were asked to separate and sit apart so we could interact with more buyers. We refused. The reps were not happy with it, but we held our ground. It wouldn't have mattered too much anyway. We fell asleep again.

The next day there was an afternoon cocktail party, a "meet-and-greet," with buyers from Belgium, Germany, Holland, and other western European countries. This was a party set up by Paramount specifically for *Laverne & Shirley*. We held a reception line as representatives from these countries passed by to greet us. I will not say which country it was, but as I was shaking hands with one gentleman he boldly announced his country would not be buying *Laverne & Shirley*. He found nothing funny about it.

I was shocked at his rudeness. I don't know what possessed me, but I said to him, "Really? Well, maybe you'll find this funny."

And as I was preparing to give him a "stage punch," Penny, overhearing this, told the surprised guest, "Just move along, buddy."

When we got back to the hotel, we went straight to bed. As I lay there in my beautiful big bed looking forward to drifting off into a comalike sleep, it came to my attention that I could hear moving around above me. It was thumping disco music and the sound of a thousand feet shaking their booties down to the ground. Evidently there was a dance club above my head. I called Penny and asked her if she could hear the music and dancing.

She said, "No." She suggested I come and sleep in her room, which I did. I ran out into the hall in my mismatched pajamas only to be greeted again by my personal butler, standing at the ready. I gave up on trying to seem appropriate. It would never happen, not even if I had been born in Paris. The ugly American smiled and entered the other ugly American's room. I fell onto a bed and slipped into a wonderful coma.

THE END OF *LAVERNE & SHIRLEY*

Laverne & Shirley ended abruptly for me. I had married Bill Hudson and was pregnant. At first there didn't seem to be a problem with me returning to the eighth season of the show. When we shot the first episode, I was four months pregnant. But when it came time to sign the contract for that season I realized that the studio had scheduled me to work on my delivery due date. I thought this was an oversight, but my attorney assured me there was no mistake. That was Paramount's schedule for the show.

I had assumed we were going to be doing wraparound shows. (This is when one actor is only in the first and last scenes of the episode and the lion's share of the show is carried by the rest of the cast.) I thought we would handle it by me working most of the shows in the beginning of the season and as I was closer to my due date, Penny would work them.

Well, I guess I had assumed wrong. In the wink of an eye, I found myself off the show. It was so abrupt that I didn't even have time to gather my personal things that I had brought from home to help decorate the set. That season my name was removed from the credits. So my eighth season of the show turned out to be my beautiful baby, Emily.

A few years later, I was doing a TV series with Telma Hopkins called *Getting By*. We shot on the Warner Brothers lot. One day, Rennie our prop man from *Laverne & Shirley* called and said he was also working on the lot, and would I meet him outside the commissary at lunch. When I arrived, Rennie wasn't there. I waited for a few minutes and then heard my name being called. I turned to see him walking toward me. He was holding Boo Boo Kitty. I started to cry. My cat had been returned because of the tender thoughtfulness of my friend, Rennie.

TEN

Outtakes

Like most of the world, I continue to be enamored with all types of talented people; be it Rodney Dangerfield, Joni Mitchell, or Shaquille O'Neal. Here are some stories of encounters and situations I have found myself in with the great and talented—named and unnamed.

THE TONIGHT SHOW

I had been entertained by Johnny Carson since he hosted *Who Do You Trust?* I can still hear my mother saying, "It should be *Whom Do You Trust?* That's the proper English! *Whom Do You Trust?*" It didn't matter who—or whom—we loved Johnny Carson and we *certainly* trusted him! When I was invited on *The Tonight Show* many years later, I was *thrilled*. I must offer a proviso here. I have not been able to review the shows I appeared in, or who the guests were alongside me. I have no personal tapes; the Internet offered little help and I could not find the shows on YouTube. The following are the general strokes to the best of my recollection.

Shirley, I Jest!

So far, I've been on *The Tonight Show* seven times. The first time was with the man *himself.* I had no idea, really, just how prepared you must be to venture out on that stage and sit in that chair next to Johnny Carson. I naively assumed it was just a question of having a fun conversation. But it was more than that, *much* more. You are out there batting with the big boys! You had to be ready with your arsenal of wit. That's what was expected of the guests on the show; seamless wit and snappy patter. I was (and had been for years) a loyal fan of Johnny Carson and *The Tonight Show*; entertained and soothed by the charm of Johnny and his guests. It comforted in the nighttime hours.

My publicist, Dick Guttman, booked me on the show. I was assigned to a segment producer. He asked me about fun things that had happened to me recently; little stories I might tell Johnny. The joke back then was if you're an actress, tell a story about your cat! At the time I did have an apartment full of kittens I was trying to find homes, I thought *maybe I could make a plea to the audience to adopt them.* But this might backfire on me because I wasn't allowed to have animals in my apartment and couldn't run the risk of my landlord seeing the show and booting me and the kittens out! No, that wouldn't be a story I could use this time. Maybe later, after I had found homes for them and was living somewhere else. But not for this show. I told my segment producer general things about my mother being a health nut and working in Bill White's Foods for Health in Van Nuys; being directed by Larry Hagman in *Return of the Blob*; failing miserably at my high school cheerleading tryouts, and of course there would be talk about *American Graffiti.* Well, let me tell you that's all well and good in theory, but when you're out there you need nerves of steel, the strength of an Olympic athlete and the presence of mind of a William F. Buckley!

I arrived at NBC Studios in Burbank and was already experiencing a case of "monkey nerves" as Penny used to refer to them. I went to makeup. Doc Severinsen was sitting in the chair next to me and greeted me so sweetly that it almost had a calming effect on me, but then I caught a glimpse of Johnny in another makeup chair. My heart began racing again. (How do people do this without being sedated first?) After makeup, I went to my producer who was waiting in my dressing room to go over my "snappy patter."

Blah, blah, blah Mama, health food. Blah, blah, blah, The Blob. Blah, blah, blah cheerleader. None of it seemed funny to me. He then invited me to wait in the Green Room. I did. It was too lonely in my dressing room. I had instructed Dick Guttman, agents, and managers to stay away—this was *not* the time to hang out! The Green Room was like the Mad Hatter's Tea Party, filled with actors and their friends and reps. I was offered a drink but declined. There was a TV mounted on the wall so you could watch the show as it progressed. I watched as the guests scored in their stories and repartee with Johnny. It neared the end of the show and looked like I was going to get bumped. Secretly I was relieved. Then all of a sudden my producer came in; pointed at me and said, "You're on!"

He led me backstage to stand by. He left me in the trusty hands of the stage manager reminding me about *Blah, blah, blah Mama, health food. Blah, blah, blah, The Blob. Blah, blah, blah cheerleader.* I don't mind confessing I was faintish. I was standing in front of a full-length mirror with a TV monitor hanging above, broadcasting the show in *real* time. The stage manager was standing there smiling at me.

Shirley, I Jest!

I gave a weak smile back and said, "Hi!"

"You look nice!" he said.

I glanced at myself at the full-length mirror. I was dressed in all brown, the only good outfit I owned at that time.

He continues, "Okay, here's how it goes. When you're announced, I pull the curtain back for you, and you'll step out on to the stage. The audience is in front of you and Johnny will be to your right. Take a bow if you like, turn right, and cross to Johnny."

"Do I kiss him or hug him?" I asked.

The stage manager took a beat to ponder as though he had never been asked this question before, "Uh, usually Johnny acknowledges you by standing, the rest is up to you. But then you go to the seat stage-right of Johnny's desk, and if the audience is still applauding you can take another acknowledgment and then sit."

"OK," I said, weakly.

"You OK?" he asked.

"Just nervous."

"Yeah, everyone is!"

I stood there during the commercial watching it on the monitor. I could see myself in the mirror, full-length, of course. The commercial was over, and all I saw now were the curtains I was supposed to step out from. Everything was backward to me! Now Johnny was saying something like: *My next guest recently starred in—*.

I stood there listening to Johnny Carson introduce me. Still watching the monitor and the curtains and glancing down to see myself in the full-length mirror. I got all turned around as though I was caught in the Bermuda Triangle. The stage manager snapped me out of it when he beckoned me to stand by him, and he prepared to pull the curtains back as Johnny finished. *Please welcome Cindy Williams.*

Doc Severinsen struck up the band to play me onto the stage. I don't remember what they played, maybe "Rock around the Clock." The stage manager said, "Here you go, and remember, Johnny's on your right!"

And with that, he pulled the curtain back. I stepped out to the audience applauding. In my head, I was saying *Johnny's on my right, Johnny's on my right! Whatever possessed me to agree to do this?*

Doc threw me a smile. I bowed, looking over to see Johnny standing. *What did the stage manager say about the hugging and kissing?* I couldn't remember, but I think I hugged him, then took my seat while the audience applause died down. Freddie de Cordova, the show's producer, was also standing as well as the affable Ed McMahon.

Johnny couldn't have been sweeter. He asked me a few questions about *American Graffiti* and if I had been a cheerleader in high school as I had played in the movie. I answered no, that I was the drill team captain. *Uh-oh!* I was at once aware of my slip-up. I had not been the drill team captain; I had been a squad leader on the drill team. I was mentally kicking myself for this *faux pas* and snapped myself out of the momentary guilt in time to respond to a question Johnny was asking. Somehow we were on the subject of *Return of the Blob.* I told Johnny that in this movie I had been eaten by the blob in a drainpipe in Glendale. This made the audience and Johnny laugh. At that moment, Johnny said,

"Well, we're out of time. Will you come back, Cindy?"

I couldn't believe it. It's every guest's dream to be asked back. Fred de Cordova and Ed McMahon were smiling at me and nodding.

"I would love to," I blurted out.

And with that Johnny thanked all his guests and the show was over. Johnny got up, said good night to everyone, and apologized to me for having so little airtime. I had scored! God bless Larry Hagman for giving me that little part. Well, everyone loved me, my family, my friends, my segment producer—so much that I was invited back for a second round with Johnny.

This time I would like to say I wasn't nervous, but that would be untrue. After makeup I was walking to my dressing room and noticed "The Amazing Kreskin" name on the dressing room door next to mine. I was a fan and had always been mesmerized by his mental genius. The door was ajar and I saw him standing there. I knocked and introduced myself and told him I was a big fan. He was delighted and thanked me. I told him I thought I was a little psychic.

He said, "Great! I'll use you in my presentation tonight!"

I immediately tried to backpedal and said that I thought it would be better if he used someone else. Why did I open my *big* mouth? He said I'd be perfect and instead of telling a long story about how I couldn't trust myself because when put on the spot I might not be clear-headed. I just said, "Thank you, but I really think it would be better if you used someone other than me."

My "snappy patter" went well enough that night. I moved down on the couch on cue. Johnny announced the Amazing Kreskin. You could tell Johnny liked him and was looking forward to whatever mentalist fete Kreskin was planning for the night. By this time I had forgotten all about being asked to participate and as Johnny was questioning Kreskin about performances he had brilliantly executed recently, he led him into saying something like, "Well, Johnny, tonight I would like to try something with you!"

Johnny was jazzed by this and Kreskin went on. "I'm going to need someone else."

"How 'bout Doc," Johnny said. Doc smiled.

"No," Kreskin said.

"I'm going to ask Cindy to help us."

"No," I blurted out, "Use Doc!"

"No," Kreskin said, turning to me. "I'd like to use you, Cindy." (I was psychic enough at that moment to know this was *not* going to end well.) Obviously Kreskin was not picking up on the thought!

If memory serves me correctly, the mental trick went something like this: Kreskin predicts, on a piece of paper, which hand Johnny will hide it in. He folds the paper and gives it to Johnny who puts his hands behind his back, placing the paper in one of them, and then holds his hands out in front of him. Kreskin asks me to predict which hand the paper is in based on his telepathic guidance.

Johnny was ready, the audience was waiting and Kreskin gave me the cue to reveal my bold prediction. Left or right? My first thought was left, then wait, oh no, right! It's the right hand. No, no, left. Definitely left. And so I boldly predicted "Right."

There was a slight pause and Kreskin asked me if I wanted to change my mind. I knew then and there my initial instinct was correct. I wrestled with myself for a nanosecond. *Which would be more embarrassing; to have guessed wrongly or if I changed my mind, the audience perhaps thinking Kreskin was signaling me in some way?* I stuck to my guns knowing I was taking the Amazing Kreskin, whose powers of mental prowess I thoroughly believed in, down into the crapper.

Johnny revealed that indeed it was his left hand that had held the paper. Kreskin revealed that he had predicted the left hand. Yet I had chosen the right.

Dear me, even while I'm writing this forty something years later, I'm humiliated! I think, *if only I'd been smarter, gotten my nursing degree, I could have avoided all this mortification!* But then again, what mistakes might I have made with my patients? No, better to take this hit publicly than mix up somebody's apple juice with their urine sample!

While we were still standing there and Kreskin was going on with his challenge I blurted out, "Well, we won't be taking *this* act to Vegas!"

No one laughed!

Later, backstage I apologized profusely to Kreskin and I have to tell you he was so gracious and self-effacing in letting me off the hook!

However, I must have done something right because Freddie de Cordova paid me the huge compliment of asking if I were interested in guest hosting *The Tonight Show*. My mind was clear, my heart rate calm and steady as I respectfully declined.

CARY GRANT

The familiar and charming voice called my name: "Cindy." Every cell in my body and mind responded with delight. I turned and in what seemed to be a beam of heavenly light stood Cary Grant. I made an audible gasp. "Well done," he continued, smiling at me. I managed a "thank you." He nodded, still smiling. Dazed, I reluctantly turned and made my way back to the table in the clubhouse at the Hollywood Park Racetrack.

I had just come up from the winners' circle where I had picked a name from a barrel to announce the recipient of a year's worth of groceries. It wasn't easy trying to get thousands of horse racing enthusiasts to quiet down long enough so I could read the winner's name. But finally the lucky family made their way from the stands to have their picture taken together with me and the winning horse and jockey. When I got back to my table, my mother and my friend, Doodles Weaver, the wonderful comic actor, were waiting for me. I was about to tell them I had just met Cary Grant when my mother shouted at a deafening decibel level, "Oh, my God, it's Cary Grant!"

I looked up to see him walking toward us. I could see my mother was about to shout out again, so I gently kicked her under the table signaling her to keep quiet. In that same moment Cary Grant arrived at our table.

"Ow! You kicked me," my mother said.

"No, I didn't!" I said demurely.

"Yes, you did!" she protested.

"No, I didn't!"

Cary Grant was standing there smiling down at us. I knew he sensed that I had indeed tried to "quiet" my mother down with a swift kick to her shin. Standing there he seemed to absolve me of my transgression. "Good afternoon, ladies!" He turned to acknowledge my mother.

Batting her eyes and offering her hand, she said, "Frances."

He took it. "Lovely to meet you, Frances."

"Lovely to meet you, Mr. Grant."

"Cary."

"Cary," she gushed.

I could see she wasn't letting go of his hand. My foot was on the ready. I considered sending another warning signal to her shin. Still holding my mother's hand, which he couldn't have let go of if he tried, it was as though she had attached herself to him with superglue! He turned to me.

"Really, Cindy, very good job out there!"

Shirley, I Jest!

"Thank you!"

"I especially liked it when you told thirty thousand people to 'Shut up!'"

I took it as a compliment and sincerely thanked him. He turned to Doodles.

"Doodles!" he acknowledged.

"Hey, Cary!" Doodles said. "Nice suit!"

He was referring to Cary Grant's white suit. I too was wearing white. It was a white pantsuit. The reason being I had read somewhere that Cary Grant wore white to the track, and that is why I chose my outfit. Kismet?

"It was lovely meeting you. Enjoy the rest of your day."

With that, Cary gracefully wrenched his hand from my mother's vicelike grip, he turned and walked away. My mother said, "My leg is going to have a bruise, you know."

MICK FLEETWOOD

I was asked to emcee a charity event honoring Mick Fleetwood of Fleetwood Mac. It was a black tie casino night affair with blackjack tables, roulette, and craps played with faux money bought by guests. All the money went to charity. The organizers were very generous and gave me a table of my own so that I could invite guests. I invited my friends Jesse, J. Sean, and Bette. It was a great event and very well put together. Everyone had lots of fun.

I waited until I had finished my duty at the microphone welcoming everyone and introducing the gala's organizer and leaving her the stage to give the charity's mission statement. I took my seat at my table with my friends and started sipping a glass of wine. I had no further duties except to help out by calling out the raffle ticket winners at the end of the night. I hadn't eaten dinner yet and was enjoying the festivities with my friends. We were all having a great time! I made a mental note: Black tie, faux gambling night—great fund-raiser!

We all strained to catch a glimpse of the fabulous Mick Fleetwood, the man of the night. He was sitting at his table directly in front of the stage. His table was filled with family and friends and like us, they were having a grand ol' time! He would receive an award later for his good works for this charity. The celebrity who would give his introduction and present him with the award had not yet arrived. I was unaware of this fact at the time and poured another glass of wine. Music played, more wine was poured as the evening went on. More speakers appeared on-stage. It was all leading up to Mick Fleetwood's introduction. I tried to grab a waiter to get a dinner plate, but had no luck.

All of a sudden the organizer appeared at my table, knelt down by me and with a cry of urgency and desperation said, "You're going to have to give the introduction for Mick."

"What?"

"The intro for Mick, Cindy, you're going to have to deliver it!"

She was in a panic and explained to me that the celebrity who was going to introduce him had not shown up yet. I told her I had had two glasses of wine on an empty stomach and I had no speech prepared.

"I'll get you a pen and a piece of paper." And she was gone! Bette, Jesse, and J. Sean all turned to me.

"I can't do this," I confessed to them with adrenaline coursing through my body.

"Sure you can," my friends rooted me on.

The organizer was back. "Cindy, we don't have time. You've got to go now! His introduction is next."

Without a pause, she swept me up like a tsunami. She led me to the stairs, up onto the stage and hurled me toward the microphone and, all the while, all eyes were on me. Damn the celebrity who was supposed to do this. Mick and his wife and guests were all smiling up at me from their table. The organizer stood to my right. I thought, *speak from your red-wine-laden heart!*

"Ladies and gentlemen," I began. "We are here tonight to honor someone." I can't remember all of my opening remarks, but they went off well enough. And when it came down to actually introducing our man of the evening and bringing him up onto the stage to accept the honor that was due to him, I remember *exactly* what I said: "Ladies and gentlemen. The best drummer in the entire universe. Fleet Micwood!" I heard it, but I didn't want to claim it! Then there was the undeniable silence in the room and Mick and his guests and family looked up at me.

"Did I just say that?" I asked my audience.

"Did I just say Fleet Micwood? Did I mention I have dyslexia?" I confessed.

The humiliation was quite uncomfortable, but the wave of the tsunami had to drop me off somewhere. "Let me try that again. Ladies and gentlemen" (my brain strained to put the "icks," "acks," and Fleet in the proper order), "the best drummer in the universe, Mick Fleetwood!" He took the stage and hugged me. He was so gracious. His table smiled at me.

J. Sean, Jesse, and Bette encouraged me by saying things like; "It was funny!" and "You were charming!"

The irony is that the celebrity scheduled to present the award showed up immediately after my debacle and delivered a great and elegant speech. Oh well, it could have been worse; I might have called him Meat Flickwood!

The organizer *never* invited me back again!

CHER

Honestly, I have no idea how we ended up there, but one Saturday in the '70s Penny and I found ourselves trying on clothes at Fiorucci's in Beverly Hills. Fiorucci's was an Italian clothing store which featured underground trends of the day such as thongs, camouflage prints, jumpsuits, gold lamé bags, and newly invented Spandex stretch jeans. A trendy clothing wonderland lined with racks and racks of hip clothes as far as the eye could see. Not much of it was Penny's nor my style, but it was great fun looking. We modeled clothes for each other, holding them up to our bodies, still on the hangers, commenting and laughing about how silly each of us looked. Then all of a sudden we spotted these black, glossy, spandex jeans. We were intrigued so we decided to try them on.

The dressing rooms at Fiorucci's were situated side by side on a little platform balcony about ten feet above the main floor. You climbed up a few stairs to get up there. While we were both thin and in very good shape thanks in part to the demanding physicality of our TV show, it still proved to be a real challenge to get those pants on. The darn things clung to your thighs no matter how petite you might be. They really should have come with a bucket of oil to help them slide on.

Penny was in the dressing room next to mine. She shouted, "I can't get these on."

"I know," I said. "I'm having trouble, too." I decided to lay down on the floor. Perhaps inertia, gravity, or sheer determination

Shirley, I Jest!

would help. I yelled back to Penny, "Try putting them on lying down!"

I yanked. I pulled. I squirmed and finally success! I had them on! The problem now was that I was lying on my back like a turtle, unable to stand. I rolled over, pushed myself up onto my hands and knees, crawled to the chair that was in the corner, grabbed onto it and, bracing myself, managed to stand.

"Penny," I shouted, "do you need help?"

"No," she replied. "If I can just get to the chair, I can hoist myself up."

I walked stiffly out of the dressing room, as did Penny. When we saw each other, we burst out laughing. Our legs looked like licorice sticks.

"I'm not getting them," she said.

"Me neither," I agreed. "We look stupid. I'll never wear them."

Just then a familiar voice chimed in from the floor below. It was Cher looking up at us. She said, "Those pants look great on you girls. You should get them."

And so we did.

The "Cher pants" hung in both of our closets for years and years, never to be struggled with again.

THE FAMOUS COOKIE

The cast of *American Graffiti* had been invited to the *Vanity Fair* Oscar party. Earlier in the year Annie Leibovitz had photographed us for the magazine and each of us had received an invitation. A week before the party I was talking with my friend Suzanne Somers. The subject of the party came up. She, of course, had been invited, too. She asked me what I was planning to wear.

Outtakes

I had already planned my trusty "big party cocktail" outfit—black cocktail pants, a black velvet jacket, a studded camisole, and all of the good jewelry I owned.

She said, "Cocktail attire, yeah that sounds right."

I assumed we were on the same page, which gave me confidence about my choice. The *Vanity Fair* party is a very exciting event and my date (one of my managers) and I were thrilled to attend. When we arrived, the paparazzi was all over Angelina Jolie, who was speaking intently with her father, Jon Voight, and her brother, James Haven. As we wended our way past them toward the entrance, a shout rang out.

"Hef! Hef! Over here!"

We turned to see Hugh Hefner with all of his lady friends on his arm. I swear it seemed like he had six girls with him and an arm for each one of them. We were almost to the door when the paparazzi shouted out again.

"Over here! Over here! This way! Right here! Look here!"

Before I could turn, I heard the thunderous sound of a thousand flashes go off.

"Over here! Look here, please!"

I turned to see Suzanne posing and flashing that beautiful smile of hers and wearing what I can only describe as a full-length, nude wedding gown with a train. Diamonds were strategically encrusted to ensure her modesty. On her head she wore a skullcap headdress reminiscent of the 1920s, with strands of diamonds hanging down, framing her face. She made Cher look like a *haus*frau. After I picked my jaw up off of the ground I went inside and waited. Suzanne and her husband, Alan Hamel, came in and started talking with a group of partygoers. I snuck up closely behind her and tapped her on the shoulder. As she turned, her diamonds swung and hit me lightly in the face.

"This is what you call cocktail attire? How much wine did you have to drink to get up the courage to wear this?"

"One glass on an empty stomach!" she laughed.

The next day, her picture in that outfit was plastered everywhere. Her daughter, Leslie Hamel, had designed it, and Suzanne wanted to wear it. Talk about marketing *genius*! Suzanne is a superb businesswoman and I've always admired her for that as well as her moxie. And I have to say, all in all it was a pretty stunning "cocktail frock"!

Meanwhile, the party was in full swing. My date had wandered off. I spotted him through the crowd, dancing up a storm. I made my way to a couch near the dance floor and took a seat so I could people watch. Tony Curtis and his wife were dancing, and I must say he was very good. A waiter was walking around with a tray of cookies, but not just *any* cookies. These had elaborate artwork. The images of different *Vanity Fair* magazine covers were artfully re-created in the icing. They were like edible party favors. By the time the waiter got to where I was sitting they were all gone. He told me he'd be back with another tray. Sitting next to me was a woman and her date. I never got her name, but we struck up a conversation. She had a big personality. I was surprised to find she wasn't an actress. We chatted for a while. I looked up and, *Oh, my goodness!* Who's this I see standing across the room? One of my favorite actors looking boyishly handsome.

I was such a huge fan, my heart starts to flutter. I'd had a major crush on him for years! We were just about to make eye contact when *whoosh*, his famous girlfriend rushes up and steals his attention away. She's a genuine beauty and a wonderful actress in her own right. Tonight she was especially dazzling in a diaphanous gown that floated to the floor. She and my "crush" started canoodling, so I turned back to my friend with the big personality. We started chatting when lo and behold I noticed she was holding one of the special cookies and I'll be darned if it wasn't my famous fella from across the way smiling up at me from the icing.

"Oh my goodness!" I told her, "Don't look up too quickly, but the icing actor on your cookie is standing across the way."

She glanced up. "So he is."

"I'm a huge fan," I told her.

"Hey, why don't you take the cookie and ask him to sign it?"

"Oh, I don't know. I think I'd be too shy and anyway, I don't have a pen."

"Here, I've got one!" And quick as a wink, she pulled a marker from her evening bag, handed it to me, and said, "Now go get that autograph, girl!"

With her encouragement, cookie and marker in hand, I start to make my way over to the actor who was now standing alone when again, *whoosh*, out of nowhere his girlfriend appeared right in front of me, right in my path.

"Where did you get that cookie?" she asked.

I was so startled that I answered as if taking an oral pop quiz. "From my friend over there," as I gestured toward the couch where my friend was now sipping a drink, watching all of this. The girlfriend kept her eyes trained on me and of course the cookie.

"I want that cookie," she said.

"Oh, I'm sorry but *I* need this cookie. I was going to ask him to sign it," I said, nodding toward the actor.

"But *I* want to give him that cookie," she stated.

"Well, really, I—." She was now standing in my personal space and I must say it was uncomfortable. She was so close that if she had any pores in her alabaster skin I could have seen them.

Shirley, I Jest!

"So, can I *have* that cookie?" she asked.

I squeezed the cookie as if it were somehow going to speak up and defend me.

"You know, truthfully," I said, "it's not mine to give." I gave a quick glance back to my friend who was now sizing up the situation. Turning back, I shifted to the right ever so slightly. She countered. She was good. If it had been a *Laverne & Shirley* episode, the writers would have had Laverne step in right about then and take her down.

I couldn't help notice how striking she was, even up close. Her hair was the kind any woman would envy. There wasn't much women wouldn't envy her for, except perhaps her lack of manners and demanding personality. I shifted to the left, this time a little more assertive. Again she countered.

When I was in college, my girlfriend Sarah had a cat, Mephisto, who possessed the same sort of agility, cunningness, and audacious behavior. He tried to kill me once. I exaggerate, but only slightly. He chased me around Sarah's apartment. We ran at speeds in that small space that could only challenge Daytona's motor speedway. Again I exaggerate, but again only slightly. He meant me harm. There was no doubt about that. I was saved only by running into the bedroom and slamming the door. And this part is no exaggeration. Mephisto ran into the door and knocked himself out.

Now, I didn't really believe this actress meant me harm, but she did intend on getting my cookie one way or another. *I can't back down*, I think. *I just can't let her have the cookie.* I glance around and saw the actor watching this scene unfold and he's laughing. Wait a minute. Is he laughing *at* me? Or at the possibility of a girl fight over his cookie? Whatever it is, all of a sudden, I'm not so enamored with him. Did they discuss this? Did she say to him, *Watch me take your cookie from that woman?*

I wanted to bite through the icing and take his head off, both literally and figuratively, but instead, I simply said, "Here." And handed her the cookie. I'm not sure if she thanked me. I didn't really care. The cookie nor the actor no longer beguiled me. I was over him.

When I returned to the couch, my friend said, "Why did you give her the cookie?"

"I can't really answer that," I said.

"I would have eaten it right there in front of her."

"Yeah, I thought about that."

"Want a drink?"

"No, I'm OK. Sorry I lost the cookie."

"That's all right, I never liked him anyway!" she said.

Tony Curtis and his wife were still dancing. This cheered me up immediately.

CIRCUS OF THE STARS

Circus of the Stars was a very popular show that began in the seventies. In one of these shows, I was asked to be co-ringmaster along with Michael York. We had been rehearsing all week and were in the middle of dress rehearsal when a break was called. I wandered off the big soundstage, which had been set up as a three-ring circus, and stood in the area outside where people were milling about in their costumes, socializing, and drinking coffee.

I noticed Lucille Ball to my left just coming off the soundstage. She had stopped for a moment in the doorway. She looked great in her outfit, a sort of leotard tuxedo with tails. She looked up and shouted at her daughter, Lucie Arnaz, who was sitting atop a huge, majestic elephant.

"Hi, honey," she said.

"Hi, Mom!" Lucie shouted back.

All of a sudden, a panicked voice shouted, "Look out, he's coming your way!"

There was a commotion—people shouting and the sound of feet running. And then the crowd to my right parted with people screaming as a chimpanzee, also dressed in a tuxedo, burst through. He was running full speed, heading straight for the soundstage door and Lucille Ball!

The chimp's trainer was in hot pursuit, screaming "Look out! Look out!" as he too burst through the crowd. The chimpanzee took no prisoners. He sped along, making a beeline toward the door. People scattered to let him pass or froze in disbelief.

"Watch yourself! Watch out," again the trainer warned as the chimp was now bearing down on his chosen target—Lucille Ball.

In an instant, Lucy was up on her toes, legs bowed, hands bracing her on each side of the door frame. *Zoom!* The chimp ran under her legs and disappeared onto the soundstage. Stunned silence. And then without missing a beat, Lucille Ball looked up at her daughter and shouted, "Lucie, whatever you do, don't let go of that elephant!"

A STUDIO CELEBRATION

Paramount was celebrating its seventy-fifth anniversary. The studio had sent invitations out requesting the presence of their stars for a group photo to be shot in the front of the iconic gates on Melrose. Years before, I had to make a bus transfer on my way to work at the International House of Pancakes on Sunset and would wait at this very site, outside these beautiful gates. Many times I would stand gazing through the ornate ironwork, down the mysterious little street and the charming two-story building that housed the wardrobe department. I would think, *Someday, someday I'm going to be on the other side of these gates.*

The invitation requested the honor of my presence and indicated the time I should arrive. My son, Zak, had just been born and I was really in the mama mode. I hadn't worked in a while and I was enjoying my time at home with my new baby, and my three-and-a-half-year-old daughter, Emily. My temperament wasn't that of a TV star going home to the studio that helped make her famous. It was more like "Isn't this nice? Wasn't it sweet of them to think of me?"

I drove myself in my car, complete with children's car seats still in the back. It would have been a chore to remove them, so I just left them in place. I had called the studio a week before asking what to wear. The answer was, "Just wear whatever you want." Whatever I want? Shouldn't there be some sort of dress code? Uniformity? Or at least a suggestion of what not to wear? It was, after all, a big Hollywood event, but they seemed nonplussed by my queries. I pulled out the best thing I could find that I felt was right for the event and would fit me after having had the baby.

It was an early afternoon affair. I worried about the traffic back into the Valley because it seemed as though we wouldn't get out of there until rush hour. But as I drove onto the lot and up to the guard gate, being received so respectfully, I must say I did have a Norma Desmond moment. The beauty of motherhood muted into the beauty of Paramount and all of the wonderful memories came flooding back (as well as old *Enquirer* headlines). I was directed to drive my car down Windsor Street to the soundstage where the event was taking place.

As I pulled my car up, I could see Paramount employees leaning out windows, waving. They were like a cheering section. Someone shouted, "Cindy, hi!"

I looked up and shouted back, "Hi!"

The attendant told me I didn't need a ticket—when I wanted my car I should just give him my name. Once on the soundstage my heart immediately began pounding. There were so many famous people.

The soundstage was not set up in a festive way, but rather bleachers and small risers scattered around. I didn't see any food or drinks, and I was looking for them.

"Cindy!" came a voice from off in the distance. I turned to see Mark Harmon. Mark had played my would-be date on *Laverne & Shirley*.

"Hi, Mark!"

Before I could say anything else, a voice from behind beckoned. I turned and there, smiling that smile at me was Tom Cruise, who I had never met. "Hi," I responded. I was sandwiched between two of the most handsome men in the world! I wanted to linger, but a topic of conversation escaped me. I turned back to Mark, but he was now speaking with someone else. I turned back around. Tom Cruise had disappeared, only to be replaced by Gene Hackman who came up and gave me a big hug. We chatted for a minute, but there was really no place to settle in.

A photographer was trying to get people up on one of the little risers that had been set up for small group shots. No one was listening. He looked at me and asked if I would be the first one up on the riser. I climbed up. In a nanosecond, so many people followed my lead that I ended up being pushed off and didn't make it into the photo.

When it came time for the picture at the front gate to be taken, an announcement was made asking everyone to please take a number out of the bowl that was perched on a table. They explained that the number you drew would correspond with a number on the riser. People swarmed to get their number. We really could have used a director or at least a camp counselor to keep us in order.

I walked up to get my number at the same time as Olivia Newton-John. Olivia asked me if I would walk with her to the gate. I was happy to have the company. I had only met her once before and even then I didn't actually meet her. She had come to the set of *Laverne & Shirley* to ask Penny and me if we would appear on her TV special. Penny and I were in my set dressing room having a bit of a squabble. Our producer tried to coax us out, but we were too embarrassed to speak to Olivia, fearing she had heard our loud voices. She had, however, stopped our squabble, but we waited for her to leave before we came out. (Very discourteous of us!)

As Olivia and I exited the soundstage onto the street and headed for the gate, John Travolta came running past us. He turned, still running, stretched out his hands and shouted, "Olivia, come with me!"

"Do you mind, Cindy?" Olivia asked.

"No," I said.

Off she ran, holding John's hand, heading toward the bleachers. Sandy and Danny running toward the Melrose gate. It was a thing of beauty.

After the photos were taken (I was standing between Matthew Broderick and Ted Danson), we all returned to the soundstage to help the president of Paramount, Frank Mancuso, blow out the candles on the huge cake that had been wheeled in. Again we were on the risers for this photo op. I stood in front of Ali MacGraw and behind Harrison Ford. They wanted to get another picture, this time of the entire group blowing out the candles. While Frank gave a speech, Ali murmured something funny. I don't remember what it was exactly, but it made me laugh. When we were asked to blow the candles out, I loudly suggested that Harrison should do it alone. He told me to shut up.

When it was finally time for me to head home, I went to get my car. To retrieve our cars, we had to wait in a tented area. We simply told them our name and they brought the car around, announcing our names over a loudspeaker so the Paramount employees—our cheerleaders—could applaud and send a rousing cheer of support as we drove off. When I got into the tented waiting area, I noticed Martha Raye and Olivia de Havilland were sitting side by side on a bench. They smiled at me and I smiled back. Olivia de Havilland was wearing a beautiful couture dress. It had been rumored she had come all the way from Paris for this event. Martha Raye was wearing a stunning red jacket over gray slacks. I was also in red. Red top, red skirt.

A handsome young actor came into the tent with a worried look on his face and started pacing dramatically. I didn't recognize him, but I asked him what was wrong. He said, "When they announce my name, I'm sure no one will cheer because no one knows who I am."

I looked over at Martha Raye and Olivia de Havilland and said, "Well, we'll cheer for you, won't we?" They each slowly nodded in agreement.

Martha Raye said, "Sure we will!" as she gave me a quizzical look as if to ask, *who is he?*

I turned and asked the young actor, "What's your name?"

"Kevin Costner," came the reply.

When Kevin's name was called, he stepped out onto the street to get into his car. Olivia de Havilland, Martha Raye, and I stood shoulder to shoulder cheering him on.

"Yay, Kevin! We love you, Kevin! Kevin, you're the greatest!"

The crowd was cheering also. He really had nothing to worry about in the first place. He looked back and tossed us a handsome smile of gratitude.

THE BARD, THE NIGHTBIRD, AND THE BOSS

I had the chance to meet Bob Dylan once in 1973. It was a busy night at Dan Tana's and I was with friends waiting for a table. Dan Tana's, a very popular restaurant in West Hollywood, is located on Santa Monica Boulevard next to the Troubador. My friend and wonderful actor Harry Dean Stanton came in and joined us. We were all talking and having fun at the bar when Harry said he had to run next door to the Troubador for a minute. Ten minutes later our table still wasn't ready. Harry returned and took me aside. "Cindy, I want you to come next door and meet Bob." Knowing that he had just worked in *Pat Garrett and Billy the Kid* with Bob Dylan, I understood who "Bob" was immediately. The level of excitement I felt took my breath away. I told Harry to wait while I gathered everyone. He gently stopped me and said, "Oh, I can't take everyone, just you." I paused and thought for a second, and then told him I didn't feel right about leaving everyone else behind. He tried to talk me into it, but I just couldn't. No, for as much as it pained me, I had to decline Harry's tempting and fantastic offer. Harry, being Harry, understood.

After he left to go back over to the Troubador, I glanced over at my friends sitting there at the bar merrily chatting and drinking their wine, while still waiting for a table, and thought, "I love you guys, and you'll never know how much." Simultaneously I wanted to bolt out the door, catch up with Harry and scream, "Screw them! Take me to Bob Dylan!" But alas, The Bard would have to wait.

Fast-forward to 1980 and the road crew from Bruce Springsteen's "The River Tour" had come down to our soundstage at Paramount to watch a rehearsal of *Laverne & Shirley*. They were great guys. And before they left, the road manager (I'll call him John because I can't remember his name, I hope he forgives me if he reads this) invited me and Penny to the concert, which was going to be at the L.A. Sports Arena. He wanted to make sure we came backstage after the show to meet "The Boss." They arranged two tickets for each of us as well as backstage passes. We were over the moon! I took my friend and writer, Kathleen Rowell. Penny took Carrie Fisher. At the concert, Kathleen and I wore our backstage passes proudly around our necks. When the incredible show ended, Kathleen and I wended our way through the crowd to find the dressing room. We found a door with a guard, showed our passes, and were allowed inside. The trouble was this area was swarming with even more people who were also wearing backstage passes. Just then, Penny and Carrie ran by.

"Penny! Penny!" I shouted. They kept traveling.

Penny shouting back over her shoulder, "We're looking for Dylan."

"Did she say they're looking for Dylan?" I asked Kathleen.

"I think so," she said.

At that moment, someone stepped between us. It was John. He put his arms around us and friendly as can be, said, "Girls, let me take you to the *real* backstage."

"This isn't it?" I asked.

"No," he replied. "Follow me."

Kathleen and I dutifully followed John through a maze of people, down a hallway, and through another door until we were in some sort of inner sanctum with dim but beautiful lighting.

"Wait here," John said. "I'll come and get you and take you in to meet Bruce."

All of these rooms reminded me of a set of nesting boxes that you keep opening one after another, each time finding a smaller box inside the other until, in the final tiny box, a gift is waiting for you. In this case the gift was Bruce Springsteen!

Kathleen and I were thrilled that we were the first ones here. We were actually giggling with delight. Then suddenly out of nowhere Kathleen blurted out, "Oh my God!"

"What?" I asked.

She was looking over my shoulder. I turned and standing there smiling at us was Bob Dylan. Kathleen became lightheaded from the sight of "The Bard" and stumbled back into a chair where she sat trying to regain her composure.

"Hi!" he said.

"Hi," I said. It seemed like the entire Mesozoic Age was passing by. I couldn't think of anything to say. And anyway, how do you strike up a conversation with Bob Dylan? There was nothing clever, wise, thought-provoking, no alliteration, poetic phrase, gushing compliment, insight, observation, personal note, or quip I could possibly come up with that hadn't already been said to this wondrous human being. And then I had it: It came to me like Haley's Comet, bright and glorious, profound and inspired. I uttered these words: "Did you have good seats?"

Bob Dylan answered, "Yes, I did."

My goodness he was charming, handsome, smiling. I couldn't remember if he was married or not, because at that moment, I *so* wanted to date him and date him bad! Just then, John came in and said, "Bob." Bob nodded, said good-bye to me and disappeared down a hall and into what I imagined was Bruce Springsteen's dressing room. I looked over to see Kathleen struggling like a turtle on its back trying to get up. I offered her my hand and I was just about to say, "Bob Dylan, Kathleen! You just missed Bob Dylan!" when she once again, gazing behind me said, "Oh my God!"

I turned to see Stevie Nicks standing in the exact same place where Bob Dylan had been. I let go of Kathleen and before I could utter a syllable, Stevie gestured to me and said, "Oh hi! It's you. I love Boo Boo Kitty!"

Poetic *and* appropriate, I thought. Then Stevie started talking to me as though we were old high school friends. Because of her music and lyrics, I certainly felt like we were friends; like I knew her well. Kathleen had managed to rise and say hi. Stevie said hi and then asked us who else was here. I told her Bob Dylan had just gone into Bruce's dressing room. She seemed as excited as me and the faintish Kathleen!

"Cindy, Kathleen!" John said, beckoning us. Saying good-bye to Stevie Nicks, we once again followed John. At that moment, Penny and Carrie rushed into the room. The thought crossed my mind to tell them that they had just missed Bob Dylan, but I didn't want to burst their bubble. Following John like the Pied Piper,

Outtakes

Kathleen and I found ourselves standing in front of "The Boss." Again, an extraordinarily talented human being who was friendly and gracious to us.

From the very first time I'd seen Bruce Springsteen perform, I couldn't take my eyes off his boots. They always seemed to be an important extension of his performance. He was wearing them tonight. And so I said, "I noticed you wear those boots a lot."

He looked at them, and then looked up and said thoughtfully, "Yeah, I like these boots."

I knew it, I just knew it! Those boots had a story.

In the car on the way home Kathleen and I discussed the boots. She said, "I think they're just boots, Cindy."

"Oh no, Kathleen, I think they are much more than just boots."

I dropped her off, making sure she got into her house safely. As I drove the rest of the way home it came to me. I should have told Bob Dylan how my father had called me into his room that day to tell me how much he liked "this singer" on TV. And how we spent those last few minutes together listening to him sing "Mr. Tambourine Man."

I think Bob Dylan would have liked that and considered it a true compliment.

Epilogue

FATHER OF THE BRIDE

Very early one morning when my son, Zak, was three years old, he woke me up. He couldn't sleep; he wanted to play. I took him downstairs into the den where his toys were, and while he sat on the floor playing, I turned on the TV. I was channel surfing when Spencer Tracy's face popped up on the screen. I stopped. I recognized the movie immediately. It was *Father of the Bride.* I had watched it so many times as a kid and I loved it. I settled in to watch it again. It was one of those movies that had everything—great story, great characters, and a great cast. It brought you in, made you a part of this family that had its foibles, flaws, poignancy, and great sense of humor.

I started thinking, this is totally relatable! It has something for everyone. A beloved daughter who's about to become a bride, two sons who respect their parents, a loving wife and mother who is exasperated with her husband, a doting husband and father who is a bit of a curmudgeon (as well as a penny-pincher).

Epilogue

As I watched the movie, and my little guy playing happily, the thought hit me! *Father of the Bride* would be a great updated remake! Another thought hit me; starring Jack Nicholson in the role of George Banks. I could see it as *plain* as day, and plain as day—it was destined to become a *hit*!

I remembered I'd read in *Variety* a week earlier that Ted Turner had acquired the MGM library of movies, and I knew just how formidable an acquisition that was. I must have seen every single film that was now in Ted Turner's possession and they were all iconic.

The next day I had the opportunity to pitch my idea to Carol Baum at Sand Dollar Productions, Sandy Gallen and Dolly Parton's company. I was meeting with Carol about an entirely different project they were producing. They were interested in me for one of the lead parts. Midway through the meeting I spoke up and told Carol that I didn't feel I was right for the part and before she could say anything I said, "May I ask you for your professional opinion about something else? What would you think about an updated remake of *Father of the Bride* starring Jack Nicholson?"

To her credit, Carol quickly replied, "Can I run with it?"

"Yes," I said, "as long as you keep me in the loop."

She promised. And we were off to the races! Over the next month I exchanged many phone calls with Ted Turner's company helping to acquire the rights from them. I must say they were some of the most courteous people I've ever encountered and with a little more back-and-forth, we prevailed and obtained the rights. Now it was time to find a studio to produce. It came in the form of Disney who hired Charles Shyer and Nancy Meyer, a husband-and-wife writing team, to rewrite an earlier version of the script. The script was sent to Jack Nicholson, but eventually Jack had to pass on it. Steve Martin ended up playing the role of George Banks and became everyone's favorite frugal father. And my hunch was right! It was a huge across-the-board hit! Thanks to Charles and Nancy's writing, Charles's direction, and an incredible cast that included Diane Keaton, the movie turned out better than I could have ever dreamed. It made millions of people delighted and happy. I was so proud in so many different ways. Thank you, Zak, for wanting to play early that morning!

CURTAIN

Oh! And by the way, when I *did* step out on stage with Gene Kelly to sing "You Wonderful You" at the Pasadena Playhouse, I hit every note. Gene was right, we sounded great together. It was a terrific duet and, aside from the fact that once again I was standing on his foot, perfect.

Acknowledgments

There are people I would like to thank who have supported me throughout the writing of this book. And to all these people I give my deep appreciation and heartfelt thanks.

My cowriter and friend, Dave Smitherman, who encouraged me for so many years and kept me calm through many storms. I would have never been able to do it without you, truly.

My tenacious literary agent, Diane Nine, who wouldn't take no for an answer. My manager extraordinaire, Arlene Forster, who always sees the glass half full even when it's empty. Jimm DiMaggio, who always had my back and typed a million words a minute with no mistakes. CBS and Lorra-Lea Bartlett, for helping me so much with the pictures, especially the cover photo. I'll get you those cupcakes, I promise. Universal, Roni Lubliner, and Diedre Thieman, for being so professional and kind. To Lynne, my BFF who can always talk me down out of the coconut tree. To Edna, for making me laugh when times were tough for both of us. To Lorie, for a treasure of high school camaraderie. And a great big kiss to my darling Ed Begley Jr. To Fred Roos, you were the beginning of it all and I will always adore you. And to Brian, for staying up later than all of us.

Acknowledgments

Suzanne Somers for being a good sport and reminding me of great stories, and Ron Howard, a great acting partner.

To Henry Winkler for always having a kind word and Harrison Ford for his quick wit.

To Emily and Zak who kept saying "don't worry, everything's going to be all right."

To Penny, whom I have always loved creating with. "Let's get together and do it again sometime."

And to Garry Marshall who I know is in Heaven writing something marvelous and mirthful, "I will always hold you in my heart with fond and happy memories."

Learn more at www.ThisIsCindyWilliams.com.